D0753965

acy Series

ON DISCOURSE ANALYSIS IN CLASSROOMS

Approaches to Language and Literacy Research

(AN NCRLL VOLUME)

David Bloome
Stephanie Power Carter
Beth Morton Christian
Samara Madrid
Sheila Otto
Nora Shuart-Faris
Mandy Smith
with contributions by
Susan R. Goldman *and* Douglas Macbeth

Teachers College, Columbia University
New York and London

NCRLL

National Conference on
Research Language and Literacy

Published by Teachers College Press, 1234 Amsterdam Avenue, New York, NY 10027

Published in association with the National Conference on Research in Language and Literacy (NCRLL). For more information about NCRLL, see *www.nyu.edu/education/teachlearn/research/ncrll*

Library of Congress Cataloging-in-Publication Data

On discourse analysis in classrooms: approaches to language and literacy research / David Bloome . . . [et al.]
   p. cm. — (Language and literary series)
 Includes bibliographical references and index.
  ISBN 978-0-8077-4914-2 (pbk.) — ISBN 978-0-8077-4915-9 (hardcover)
1. Language and education. 2. Discourse analysis. I. Bloome, David.
401'.41—dc22   2008013680

ISBN 978-0-8077-4914-2 (paperback)
ISBN 978-0-8077-4915-9 (hardcover)

Printed on acid-free paper
Manufactured in the United States of America

15 14 13 12 11 10 09 08   8 7 6 5 4 3 2 1

Contents

From the NCRLL Editors

A book that promises its readers new ways of "seeing" language and literacy events in classrooms is intriguing on several fronts. First, it suggests that such events are rarely what they seem to be on first glance. Second, it implies that approaches to researching classroom language and literacy events are not set in stone—that they vary with the researcher. Third, it hints at new insights that can be gleaned from looking and then looking again. *On Discourse Analysis in Classrooms* delivers on its promise. The authors have written this book for researchers who are interested in exploring discourse analysis frameworks that move beyond isolated approaches to studying the dynamics of language and literacy events in everyday classrooms.

Perhaps most fascinating of all is the authors' successful bid to take readers up close to language in use. Starting with a single classroom literacy event, they apply different discourse analyses of that event for the express purpose of showing that multiple— even contradictory—interpretations are possible. These framings are far from relativistic, however. In fact, the authors carefully lay out a process for creating productive tensions among the different interpretations that can lead to more in-depth understandings of classroom language and literacy events and a greater appreciation of the affordances and limitations of discourse analysis as employed in this book.

On Discourse Analysis in Classrooms is the sixth volume in the National Conference on Research in Language and Literacy (NCRLL) collection of books published by Teachers College Press. These volumes, written by prominent researchers in the field, offer insights, information, and guidance in understanding and employing various approaches to researching language and literacy. The first five well-received books are *On Qualitative Inquiry* by George Kamberelis and Greg Dimitriadis; *On the Case* by Anne Haas Dyson and Celia Genishi; *On Formative and Design Experiments* by David Reinking and Barbara Bradley; *On Ethnography* by

Shirley Brice Heath and Brian V. Street; and *On Critically Conscious Research* by Arlette Willis, Helena Hall, Mary Montovan, Catherine Hunter, LaTanya Burke, and Ana Herrera. Subsequent books in this collection will include approaches to language and literacy research in teacher inquiry by Dixie Goswami, Ceci Lewis, Marty Rutherford, and Diane Waff; narrative inquiry by David Schaafsma and Ruth Vinz; mixed methods by Robert Calfee and Melanie Sperling; and quantitative research methods by P. David Pearson and Barbara Taylor.

The "On . . ." books: where language and literacy researchers turn to learn. Welcome to the conversation.

—*JoBeth Allen* and *Donna E. Alverman*

Acknowledgments

We appreciate the opportunity that the National Conference on Research on Language and Literacy (NCRLL) and series editors, JoBeth Allen and Donna Alvermann, have given us to write this book. We hope this volume contributes to their vision of a field where scholars from diverse disciplinary backgrounds, methodological approaches, and experiences celebrate the eloquence and contribution of different epistemologies and logics-of-inquiry.

Susan Goldman and Doug Macbeth generously gave their time and wisdom to this volume by adding special contributions to Chapter 3. They joined Stephanie Carter and Mandy Smith in composing illustrations of how discourse analysis might be conducted from differing perspectives. We are honored to include their voices in this book.

We owe a special acknowledgment to Judith Green who continued to challenge our ideas and encouraged us to write the book in a manner that would provoke the imagination of the field of research in language and literacy. We also owe special acknowledgment to Caroline Clark who read through an early version of the book manuscript and provided feedback on conceptual issues and writing and helped us make connections with the work of other scholars. We acknowledge and are appreciative of the feedback provided by Cynthia Lewis, Ellen McIntyre, and Betsy Rymes, who reviewed an earlier version of the manuscript for NCRLL. Mariela Herrara and Caitlin Ryan provided feedback on clarity and style.

We want to acknowledge comments on earlier versions of this book provided by Laurie Katz, Carol Lee, Jerrie Willett, and students in two doctoral courses on literacy, language, and culture and on discourse analysis at The Ohio State University. Mollie Blackburn provided insights and directions for key theoretical issues. Ari Bloomekatz provided clerical assistance, managing and coordinating reviews and checking style issues. Whatever flaws and shortcomings remain are our sole responsibility.

Some of the discussion in this book has been inspired by *Discourse Analysis and the Study of Classroom Language and Literacy Events: A Microethnographic Perspective* (2005) authored by David Bloome, Stephanie Power Carter, Beth Morton Christian, Sheila Otto, and Nora Shuart-Faris.

We also want to express our gratitude to The Ohio State University, Indiana University, Tennessee State University, and Middle Tennessee State University, our academic and intellectual "homes," which provided us with the space and opportunity to work on this book. (The views and opinions expressed here do not necessarily reflect the policies of the institutions noted here.)

—*David Bloome, Stephanie Power Carter,*
Beth Morton Christian, Samara Madrid,
Sheila Otto, Nora Shuart-Faris, Mandy Smith
February 2008

Introduction

The students in a ninth-grade language arts class have just read Alice Walker's short story, "Everyday Use." Midway through the subsequent discussion of the story, the teacher has the following exchange with Valerie:

> *Teacher:* So what kind of a person is Dee?
> *Valerie:* She wants to be something she's not
> *Teacher:* OK she wants to be something she's not Ummmmm. because she wants nice things or or wha why why do you say that

What is to be made of this interaction among students and teacher? How shall it be analyzed? How compared? Within what frameworks? From which perspectives? With what logic-of-inquiry? How shall it be contextualized? How embedded in the broader social event? In other events? Should it be viewed as an iteration of broader social processes? Of cognitive processes? Of the particularities of the local settings? How can multiple perspectives be brought to bear upon this classroom literacy event? Can such a small bit of data be useful in generating new insights about language and literacy in classrooms more generally? And if so, how? What questions should and can be legitimately asked of such an interaction and how should they be asked?

This book provides an introductory discussion of discourse analysis of language and literacy events in classrooms. Interest in the use of discourse analysis by educational researchers has increased over the past few decades. Part of the interest in discourse analysis is due to the attention that discourse analysis places on the details of people interacting with each other in their daily lives. Discourse analysis allows researchers to get very close to what people actually do in literacy events in classrooms. And it is by getting very close to what people actually do in literacy events such as the exchange above that educators and researchers can build compelling, explanatory theories about classroom processes, social processes, reading, writing, and learning as they occur in classrooms.

From the very beginning you should know that this book does not attempt to represent all perspectives or approaches to discourse analysis. Nor is this book a "how-to" book for conducting discourse analysis. There already exist many excellent introductory books that do such things (see Supplemental Bibliographies). Rather, the purpose of this book is to introduce approaches to discourse analysis in a way that provokes the imagination of educational researchers interested in literacy events in classrooms, even if they never themselves engage in discourse analysis studies. That is, our effort in this book is to position discourse analysis as ways to redefine traditional topics of study related to literacy events in classrooms. For us, discourse analysis is not a set of methods per se but a set of ways of "seeing" language and literacy events in classrooms.

Approaching Discourse Analysis

One defining characteristic of discourse analysis studies is that the construct of discourse is central to both the theoretical framing and to the logic-of-inquiry employed. Yet, many authors of discourse analysis studies either do not specify their definitions of *discourse* or *discourse analysis* or give vague definitions. They assume an unarticulated shared understanding of underlying constructs and a logic-of-inquiry (see Titscher, Meyer, Wodak, & Vetter, 2000, for a rare example of a detailed definition). As a result, many people find reading discourse analysis studies a frustrating experience.

As we discuss throughout the book (and especially in Chapter 2), there are many definitions of discourse. These include definitions of discourse closely tied to language use, texts, and face-to-face social interaction, as well as definitions of discourse associated with ways of being, regimes of knowledge, and the structures of social institutions. There are definitions of discourse as a thing in and of itself (what we call definitions of discourse as a noun) and definitions of discourse as actions people take with regard to each other and the worlds in which they live (what we call discourse as a verb). Perhaps it is as Van Dijk (1997) states, that "the notion of discourse is essentially fuzzy" (p. 1).

It is our view that whatever definition of discourse one holds it should be held loosely with acknowledgment of the contribution of other definitions and with anticipation of being able to layer the insights from the use of multiple definitions of discourse (what we call *laminating* and discuss in Chapter 4). Although we will discuss various definitions of discourse in this book, we want to make clear how we define discourse in many of our studies (see Bloome et al., 2005, for more detailed discussion). The particular definition of discourse we use is captured by Bloome and Clark's (2006) term *discourse-in-use* (although we do not use that term in this book).

> The concept of discourse-in-use is a helpful heuristic to distinguish the focus here from other definitions of discourse. Discourse has been defined as ways, aesthetics, styles, and structures of using language and written text as a set of cultural, historical, and ideological processes, among other definitions. . . . people use language and other semiotic tools within multiple layers of social context, and [those] ways of using language do not exist distinct from broader social and historical processes. We use discourse-in-use to ask who is using language and other semiotic tools to do what, with whom, to whom, when, where, and how? The concept of discourse-in-use focuses attention on how people adopt and adapt the language and cultural practices historically available in response to the local, institutional, macro social, and historical situations in which they find themselves. (p. 209)

Reading discourse analysis studies can also be frustrating because there is no simple list of criteria that can distinguish a good discourse analysis study from a bad one nor is there a simple list of questions that discourse analysis studies can answer and cannot answer. Nor can one simply ask, "Is the study useful?" as if *usefulness* was easy to define. One way to approach the usefulness of discourse analysis studies of classroom language and literacy events is to ask questions such as:

- Does the discourse analysis help us understand literacy events in classrooms in new ways and lead us to ask new questions?

- Does it help us redefine some of the theoretical constructs in our field(s)?

Or we might ask more specific questions:

- What entry points for understanding literacy events in classrooms in new ways does a discourse analysis study provide?
- What entry points does it provide for understanding our disciplinary and professional fields in new ways? How does it provide those entry points?

Answering such questions is not necessarily a summative or synergistic process; rather, it entails a dialectical process focused on generating new definitions of classrooms, literacy events, practices, and processes, and reflexively redefining discourse analysis.

THREE-WAY GAZE OF DISCOURSE ANALYSIS STUDIES

In our view, with regard to underlying theoretical principles and epistemological assumptions, a discourse analysis study of language and literacy events in classrooms should always look in at least three directions (see Figure I.1): related disciplines; the nascent history of other discourse analysis studies of language and literacy events (conducted both in classrooms and elsewhere); and the social problem being addressed (what is called "problem-based research," cf. Green & Bloome, 1997).

To briefly elaborate Figure I.1, a discourse analysis study of language and literacy events in classrooms may reflect and refract various disciplines to which it is related. It borrows concepts, terms, and interpretive principles from one or more disciplinary fields. In our own work, we have found it useful to employ concepts and terminology from multiple fields including linguistics (e.g., Duranti & Goodwin, 1992; Fairclough, 1992, 2003; Fillmore, 1997; Goodwin, 1981; Hanks, 1996; Schiffrin, 1987, 2006; Tannen, 2007), anthropology (e.g., Bauman, 1986; Geertz, 1973, 1983), literary studies (e.g., Bakhtin, 1935/1981, 1953/1986; Bakhtin & Medvedev, 1978; Volosinov, 1929/1973), the ethnography of communication (e.g., Gumperz, 1986; Hymes, 1974), social theory (e.g.,

Figure I.1. Three-way gaze of discourse analysis studies of language and literacy events in classrooms.

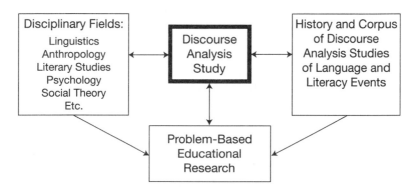

Bourdieu, 1977; Bourdieu & Thompson, 1991; de Certeau, 1984; Foucault, 1965, 1972, 1980; Giddens, 1979; Smith, 1987), theories of space and time (e.g., Adam, 1990; Gell, 1992; Leander & Sheehy, 2004; Soja, 1996), cognitive science (e.g., Bransford et al., 1999; Bransford, Brown & Cocking, 1999; Frederiksen, 1989; Goldman, 1997, 2003) and sociohistorical psychology theory (e.g., Gonzalez, Moll & Amati, 2005; Vygotsky, 1987; Wertsch, 1993). Given the broad range of disciplinary fields from which scholars engaged in discourse analysis draw, one could claim that discourse analysis is inherently a multidisciplinary and interdisciplinary field. However, it is not just a matter of borrowing terminology and reflecting the disciplines; rather, the borrowing is accompanied by a challenge to those same disciplinary fields with regard to the units of analysis employed, the extension and redefining of key concepts and principles, the incorporation of other disciplines, an orientation to being "problem-based" research, and a grounding in field study and in the lived experiences of the people in the events studied.

The second direction in which a discourse analysis study of language and literacy events in classrooms looks is toward previous related discourse analysis studies of language and literacy events. There has been an extensive set of discourse analysis studies of classroom language and literacy events. Any new discourse analysis study of classroom literacy events should acknowledge the insights, perspectives, and framings of pertinent previous studies. One way that discourse analysis studies build a knowledge base is by generating new perspectives and understandings and then "laminating" those perspectives with extant perspectives and findings (see Chapter 4 for a discussion of laminating).

A third direction in which a discourse analysis study of language and literacy events in classrooms looks is toward a field-based "problem" that defines the need for the study. A *field-based problem* is a need, condition, threat, trouble, dilemma, crisis, difficulty, or opportunity that exists among people in their lived experiences. Field-based problems may result from a lack of social justice and educational equity, from historical circumstances, from geographic and natural conditions, from inadequate and underdeveloped educational processes and resources, from a lack of knowledge, or from some combination of these. A field-based problem may be associated with pain and suffering, but a field-based problem may also be an opportunity for re-creation and reconstruction, building new social relationships, transforming social institutions, and creating opportunities for social solidarity and caring relationships. The centrality of a field-based problem to educational research is one dimension that distinguishes it from discipline-based research. We take the a priori position that although identification and articulation of field-based problems may be enhanced by disciplinary knowledge and previous studies, these problems are not defined by disciplines or previous studies. They take shape and are experienced by people in their everyday lives. By definition, problem-based research calls upon the researcher to bring to bear upon the problem whatever intellectual tools disciplines and previous studies may provide, but to subordinate those intellectual tools to addressing the problem as people experience it. This requires an engagement with people's everyday lives, with how they interact with each other and with the world around them, acting on their world as it acts on them. Necessarily, problem-based research requires a dialectical relationship among the research study, disciplinary fields, previous studies, and the lived experiences of people in the events being studied. The importance of change as an underlying assumption is captured by Hymes (1974) quoting Mao Tse-Tung: "If you want to know a certain thing or a certain class of things directly, you must personally participate in the practical struggle to change reality, to change that thing or class of things" (p. 209).

LANGUAGE AND LITERACY EVENTS

This book focuses specifically on discourse analysis of language and literacy events in classrooms. Although much of the discussion in the book may apply to the study of other kinds of social events too, we have framed the discussion of discourse analysis in terms of the study of language and literacy events. Therefore, we believe it is important to discuss how we define *language, literacy,* and *social event*. How language, literacy, and social event are defined influences the conduct of a discourse analysis study while simultaneously the conduct and progress of a discourse analysis study influences how language, literacy, and social event get defined (see Figure I.2 below).

Our view of this reciprocal relationship between method or, more accurately, the logic of inquiry (cf. Birdwhistell, 1977; Green, Dixon, & Zaharlick, 2003) and the object of study derives from Bakhtin and Medvedev's (1928/1978) discussion of literary scholarship:

> From the neo-Kantian point of view it is not the method which adapts to the real existence of the object, but the object which obtains the whole individuality of its existence from the method: it becomes definite reality only in those categories which help the methods of cognition fill it out. In the object itself there is no de-

Figure I.2. Reciprocal influences of definitions of language and literacy events and conduct of discourse analysis.

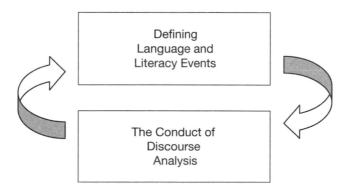

Defining Language and Literacy Events

The Conduct of Discourse Analysis

finitiveness which would not be definitive of cognition itself....
Method must of course be adapted to the object. (pp. 76–77)

The relationship between method and the object of study is a
much larger issue than can be addressed here. Suffice it to say
that this issue is a key aspect, for us, in how discourse analysis
studies of language and literacy events in classrooms are framed.
As such, it requires us to make clear how we are defining the object of study – language and literacy events in classrooms—and
to acknowledge that definitions and methods constantly evolve
within and across studies. More simply stated, from this perspective methods are always a work in progress.

Social Event

A *social event*[1] is any occurrence involving people acting and
reacting to each other. Although seemingly a simple notion, its
unpacking shows it to be complex. First, it is *people* who are acting and reacting to each other. Thus, the basic analytic unit is not
an individual, but a group of people; people are the context for
each other (cf. Erickson & Shultz, 1977). Second, people *act* and
react.[2] People react to actions immediately previous, to actions
that occurred sometime earlier, and to sets, groups, and patterns of action. People also react to future actions. Any action or
reaction inherently includes within it a concept of consequence.
Consequences presume future actions either by others or by oneself. As such, a "nonaction" can be a reaction. Third, the actions
and reactions people take to each other are not necessarily lin-
ear. People may act together and actions and reactions may occur
simultaneously. Fourth, people may act and react to each other
through sequences of actions and not just through individual actions. And fifth, meaning and significance are located in the actions and reactions people take to each other, not in abstracted or
isolated psychological states. Inasmuch as there is no separation
of people from events, there can be no separation between meaning, significance, and action. We are not saying that people do not
think about and reflect on the meaning and significance of actions
and events, but rather we assert that such thinking and reflection
are part of a social event and are formed by social relationships,
language, and history.

People in interaction with each other need to create and make visible a working consensus about what it is they are doing and how what they are doing is contextualized if they are to communicate effectively and accomplish their interactional goals. In brief, if they do not have a working consensus about what is happening, their communication will lack coherency and they will disintegrate as a group of people in interaction with each other. It can be easy to build a working consensus. For example, a teacher might say to her students, "Today we are going to continue in reading group what we were doing yesterday." And assuming that the students remember the previous day and have an understanding of that previous day similar to the teacher's, and assuming that they agree to the teacher's proposal, both the students and the teacher will have established an initial working consensus for what is happening. The students might signal their understanding of and agreement to the teacher's proposal about what is happening by moving to the appropriate chairs, opening their books, or otherwise acting in ways consistent with the teacher's proposal.

At other times, however, it takes a great deal of work to establish a working consensus about what is happening in an event. For example, consider the first day of school for a teacher and a group of students who do not know each other, who have no collective history, and who come from different educational experiences and histories. The teacher cannot simply reference a previous shared event. If the teacher remarked that the students should "open up their books and read," the students may not share a working consensus about what that means: Some might get their own books, others might look for a textbook, still others might leave to go to the library; some might start reading aloud, others silently; some might share a book; and some might do nothing because they did not recognize that the teacher had given a directive. The teacher will have to make visible what the working consensus is and will have to seek visible indications from the students that they understand. But it may also be the case that the teacher may not necessarily be able to create the specific working consensus she or he wants. Perhaps there are students in the class who view reading to the teacher as something done only after one is able to perform the oral reading perfectly. As the teacher and students interact with one another they will be negotiating and making visible to each other a working consensus about what is happening, about how significance and meaning are assigned to various actions, and what norms for interpreting, talking, acting, thinking, believing, evaluating, and feeling are shared and expected (cf. Goodenough's 1981 definition of culture).

Language

Throughout this book we continuously refer to language events rather than language, per se. A language event is any social event in which language is nontrivial to that event. Most events in our lives are language events (especially if one has a broad definition of language as not just constituted by words, but also of nonverbal language, prosody, pictorial forms, and the symbolic manipulation of materials).

Our definition of language event builds on a definition of language derived from Volosinov (1929/1973) and Bakhtin (1935/1981, 1953/1986; Bakhtin & Medvedev, 1928/1978). They propose a philosophy of language distinct from both abstract objectivism and psychologism. Abstract objectivism views language as a linguistic system distinct from how people actually use words and utterances. It is a system located neither in people nor in the social world; it exists only as a formalism. From the perspective of language as an abstract idealism, how people actually speak and write is not language but an external manifestation of language. By contrast, Volosinov (1929/1973) argues:

> The actual reality of language-speech is not the abstract system of linguistic forms, not the isolated monologic utterance, and not the psychophysiological act of its implementation, but the social event of verbal interaction implemented in an utterance or utterances.
>
> Thus, verbal interaction is the basic reality of language. . . .
>
> *Any utterance*, no matter how weighty and complete in and of itself, *is only a moment in the continuous process of verbal communication.* But that continuous verbal communication is, in turn, itself only a moment in the continuous all-inclusive, generative process of a given social collective. . . . *Verbal communication can never be understood and explained outside of this connection with a concrete situation. . . .* In its concrete connection with a situation, verbal communication is always accompanied by social acts of a

nonverbal character (the performance of labor, the symbolic acts of a ritual, a ceremony, etc.). . . . *Language acquires life and histori-cally evolves precisely here, in concrete verbal communication, and not in the abstract linguistic system of language forms, nor in the indi-vidual psyche of speakers.* (pp. 94–95, emphasis in original)

Any word or utterance needs to be understood within the context of people acting and reacting to each other and as reflecting and refracting previous events.

As an aside, we note that the use of language itself is an action (cf. Austin, 1962; Volosinov, 1929/1973), it is something people do to each other and to themselves and is part of the way that they act on the situations in which they find themselves. The view of language as action is especially important to some of the defini-tions of discourse that we discuss in Chapter 2.

Literacy

Our definition of *literacy* builds from our definition of lan-guage; throughout the book we do not refer to literacy as a stand alone, decontextualized, autonomous process but rather use the term *literacy event*. A literacy event is any social event involving nontrivial uses of written language and related semiotic systems (cf. Heath, 1982). The focus, therefore, is not on a set of skills, cog-nitive processes, or competencies that may constitute literacy, but on the ways in which written language is actually used in particu-lar events.

For example, consider the use of written language in the event represented in the brief exchange with which we began this intro-duction.

Teacher: So what kind of a person is Dee?
Valerie: She wants to be something she's not
Teacher: OK she wants to be something she's not Ummmmm. because she wants nice things or or wha why why do you say that

The students had been reading a short story and were discuss-ing it, prompted by questions from the teacher. The written lan-guage they were using included the photocopied story they had on their desks, the notes they had written on the printed text, and a list of comments and notes that had previously been written on the white board about name changes and various language arts matters. They also had available to them (although not physically present) essays they had written and shared about the nature of people changing their names. Written language is central to this social event.

When the teacher asks the students, "So, what kind of a person is Dee?" she is beginning a literacy practice with which they have already become familiar even though it is only the third week of school. They must provide an answer to the teacher which the teacher finds acceptable. In this specific event, the teacher has instructed the class to provide an answer and then read from the short story a passage providing evidence to support their response. That instruction makes this particular event a bit different from previous similar instructional conversations. Students have to use written language in a different way than they have used it in similar events in this classroom. Doing so does not appear to be difficult for the students as they are able to provide responses acceptable to the teacher. But in the particular transcript lines above, another variation occurs that is particular to these people at that particular time and place. Valerie offers a response. Valerie is extremely shy and rarely volunteers an answer. While not disliked by her peers, she does not appear to have made any friends in the class, and faces a series of difficult problems outside of school. On a previous day, Valerie had presented a collage regarding her identity that was depressing. The teacher is aware of all of this. We would argue that all of the specific circumstances just listed—and more—are part of the context of this three-line classroom interaction, and it is difficult to conduct a discourse analysis of this event without some knowledge of the context. Although we do not know what the teacher's intention was in how she responded to Valerie, just as others in the classroom can assign a set of potential meanings to the teacher's response based on their history in the classroom, as researchers we can do the same. And, like others in the classroom, we can refine the more likely potential meanings by examining subsequent interactions that give cues as to how Valerie, the teacher, or others in the classroom have interpreted the teacher's response. The teacher begins by validating Valerie's answer, then, giving one rationale for the answer, she asks Valerie to elaborate. Validating Valerie's answer is not consistent with the instructions the teacher had given for how to respond, nor is there a passage in the short story that would support such an answer; yet, other social processes may have been going on here besides helping the students acquire a way to relate to written language (which might be called making a text-based argument).

Written language is central to this brief interaction, but it is not reducible to a set of decontextualized skills or processes. Thus we define literacy as literacy events rather than as a set of autonomous processes. Given this definition of literacy, individuals may acquire increasing communicative competence and acumen[3] for participating in a type of literacy event or in a broad range of types of literacy events, which might be called literacy practices (cf. Street, 1984, 1995). From this perspective, educational processes are defined as ways of helping people acquire such acumen, including critical processes for critiquing the nature and consequences of extant literacy practices and inventing new literacy practices (cf. Street, 1996). Such a view of literacy and literacy education focuses attention on people's participation in literacy events over time, within and across classrooms, community and institutional contexts; and defines *literacy learning* as a change in participation by an individual or a group in a set of social practices over time;[4] including a change in the nature and structure of literacy practices as a consequence of people's acting upon extant literacy practices. Street (1993) summaries this focus as literacy practices acting on people and people acting on literacy practices.

ORGANIZATION OF THE BOOK

We have written this book to be of use to researchers of language and literacy in classrooms who are unfamiliar with discourse analysis and for those who have some knowledge of discourse analysis but seek additional insight and a way to frame various approaches to discourse analysis of literacy events in classrooms. For those readers who have limited knowledge of discourse analysis, we hope that this book will generate new questions to ask about literacy events in classrooms and that it will also provide you with one way to frame the affordances offered by discourse analysis studies. We strongly advise those unfamiliar with discourse analysis to read multiple introductory books on the topic and recent handbooks on discourse analysis and discourse processes. For those who have some knowledge of discourse analysis and are interested in exploring the possibilities of conducting discourse analysis studies, we hope that this book will help move you one step closer to that goal. We hope that we have written this book in a way that invites you into the field and that encourages you to bring with you your experiences and expertise in researching literacy events from other perspectives and integrate them with the constructs, findings, logics-of-inquiry, and insights that discourse analysis studies have provided. Finally, for those who already have expertise in discourse analysis and are engaged in conducting discourse analysis studies of literacy events in classrooms, we hope that you will may find this book of interest in how it "maps" the diversity of approaches to discourse analysis.

We begin in Chapter 1 by framing discourse analysis within the linguistic turn in the social sciences. By this we emphasize that discourse analysis studies are not an isolated set of techniques or methods but rather are part of a broader intellectual agenda seeking to understand how the use of language has created and defined human experience. As we have noted earlier, our view of language is an expansive one including verbal, nonverbal, and prosodic communication, related semiotic systems (e.g., graphics, pictures) as well as the manipulation of objects for the purpose of communication. Also in Chapter 1 we introduce the concepts of micro and macro levels of analysis and social and historical contexts

In Chapter 2 we discuss variations in definitions of discourse focusing on discourse as a noun and discourse as a verb as two broad heuristic categories for understanding variation in definitions of discourse and approaches to discourse analysis.

In Chapter 3 we present four different discourse analyses of the same classroom literacy event. One purpose of these multiple analyses is to emphasize variation in approaches to discourse analysis; a second purpose is to emphasize the coexistence of valid multiple interpretations (even contradictory interpretations) of the same literacy event.

In Chapter 4 we discuss how the four analyses in Chapter 3 might be brought together (what we call *laminating*). As a process, laminating creates productive tensions leading to new understandings both of literacy events in classrooms and of discourse analysis itself.

In preparation for writing this book, we reviewed a large number of books and articles on discourse analysis. In so doing, we encountered those who hold a singular definition of discourse and discourse analysis and who position themselves as having the "truth" about discourse analysis: They will be unhappy with this book. We have also come across those who hold a relativistic position, who view all definitions and approaches to discourse analysis and to research in general as equally good and important and who go no further than to celebrate diversity of perspective: They also will be unhappy with this book because we argue against such relativism. (For a detailed critique of the relativist position see Street, 1996.) In contrast to both of these positions, we argue for a dialectical process in which multiple perspectives of discourse analysis are set against each other as a means for opening up the research imagination and redefining traditionally understood constructs and processes related to language and literacy events in classrooms.

Notes

1. A detailed discussion of events as a unit of analysis can be found in Bloome, Carter, Christian, Otto, and Shuart-Faris (2005). The discussion here builds on that discussion.

2. Our use of "react" is similar to and based in part on Bakhtin's (1935) and Volosinov's (1929) discussion of "response."

3. By "acumen" we mean both appropriate, effective participation in a social event as well as being able to adapt and transform the social event to address new goals, situations, social relationships, and agendas, in an effective manner.

4. This definition of learning is informed by definitions of learning from Lave, 1996; Lave and Wenger, 1991; and Rogoff, 2003.

CHAPTER 1

Framing Discourse Analyses of Language and Literacy Events in Classrooms

As noted in the introduction, we view discourse analysis as part of broader intellectual movements in the social sciences. Discourse analysis is not a set of decontextualized, ideologically neutral, and autonomous analytical tools that can be applied to any situation or phenomena. Rather, like any approach to research, discourse analysis carries with it an ideology, its own set of intellectual framings that foreground some social processes and background or make others invisible. Discourse analysis is less a methodology than a set of ways for "seeing" language and literacy events in classrooms.

Understanding discourse analysis, in our view, needs to begin by locating discourse analysis within four broad frames:

1. The linguistic turn in the social sciences
2. The foregrounding of local events and their relationships to broader cultural and social processes (i.e., micro and macro level approaches)
3. Recognition of the importance of social and historical contexts
4. Recognition that discourse processes always involve power relations

The four frames listed above are not the only ways researchers have framed their discourse analysis studies. They also have framed their approaches to discourse analysis in terms of a disciplinary perspective (e.g., cognitive, sociological, literary), a set of social relationships among researchers and the people studied (see Potter, Wetherell, Gill, & Edwards, 1990), or in other ways. Nonetheless, we find it useful to frame discourse analysis in terms of the four frames list above even if later one decides to add additional framings or to defenestrate one or more of the framings. Given the introductory nature of this book, we only discuss these issues briefly.

Discourse Analysis and the Linguistic Turn in the Social Sciences

We view discourse analysis as grounded in the linguistic turn in the social sciences. The linguistic turn in the social sciences recognizes that language is implicated in constructions of knowledge, in configurations of cultures and cultural processes, in power relations, and in relationships among nation-states (including colonialism), classes, ethnic and racial groups, genders, sexual identities, and so on. Language creates categories of in-groups and "others," and privileges particular definitions and ways of knowing. The linguistic turn focuses the attention of social scientists and educational researchers on the language of representation, the use of language to do things, and the nature of the language of research itself. The language used to describe people, places, and actions encodes power relationships and can make hierarchy appear "natural" and "reasonable" and make invisible the pain, suffering, and lack of freedom and dignity people may experience. (For discussions of the linguistic turn in the social sciences see Agar, 1994; Atkinson, 1990; Clifford & Marcus, 1986; Geertz, 1973; Habermas, 1984, 1987; Rhorty, 1967; Said, 1979, 1985).

With regard to our interest in understanding language and literacy events in classrooms, the linguistic turn in the social sciences foregrounds how language (and related semiotic processes) is used for the following purposes:

- To construct social realities of the daily lives of students, teachers, and others, including classrooms and

educational settings related to classrooms (including
family and community settings)
- To construct relationships among individuals, groups,
  social institutions, and political entities, including
  students, teachers, parents, ethnic groups, businesses,
  churches, and government
- To construct and exercise relations of power among
  people, groups, and social institutions
- To create and exchange economic, social, cultural,
  political, and symbolic capital
- To define and create knowledge, including academic
  knowledge, disciplinary knowledge, pedagogical
  knowledge, and everyday world knowledge
- To define and constitute research including educational
  studies and discourse analysis studies

Each of the statements above assumes a view of language as a
material presence to which others need to respond (cf. Volosinov,
1929/1973). A child who is asked a question by a teacher must
respond even if the response is to decline to answer, ignore the
question, or treat the question as a statement. Stated in different
terms, when one person uses language—whether that language
is verbal, nonverbal, paralinguistic, spoken, written, electronic, or
otherwise—that person has acted on and with others. Although
there may be many ways to respond to that act, a response is necessary and inherent. As Volosinov states:

> Every ideological sign is not only a reflection, a shadow of real-
> ity, but is also itself a material segment of that very reality. Every
> phenomenon functioning as an ideological sign has some kind
> of material embodiment, whether in sound, physical mass, color,
> movements of the body, or the like. In this sense, the reality of the
> sign is fully objective and lends itself to a unitary, monistic, ob-
> jective method of study. A sign is a phenomenon of the external
> world. Both the sign itself and all the effects it produces (all those
> actions, reactions, and new signs it elicits in the surrounding so-
> cial milieu) occur in outer experience. (p. 11)

Consider what occurs when the ninth-grade language arts
teacher (described in the introduction) asks Michael to read a passage aloud from Alice Walker's short story "Everyday Use." The

other members of the class are sitting at their desks, a copy of the story in front of them. The teacher is looking at Michael and has created a pause in the flow of talk that Michael is to fill by responding to her request. Michael must address the material situation in which he finds himself. The silence, the eye gazes, the words that have already been spoken, the seating and postural configurations of the other students and the teacher, and the shared text of the short story (and its location within a sequence of texts the class has read) are all part of the material reality with which Michael is confronted. He can expect the teacher and the students to react to him regardless of what he does, whether his response is to orally render the text in a smooth flowing style, a halting basalese style, in hip-hop rhythm, or to ignore the request (to ignore is also a response). How the teacher and the other students might react will vary, but Michael can be certain that they will react. Their reaction to Michael's response will be an interpretation of what he has done, who he is (within the context of that situation), and the social significance of what he has done. In sum, as researchers study the literacy event and classroom in which Michael finds himself, they must attend to the complexities and subtleties of how people use language to act and react to each other.

It is important to note that research and researchers do not stand aloof from linguistic considerations similar to those described above in analyzing the literacy event with Michael and his ninth-grade classroom. The conduct of research itself involves the use of language and can itself be characterized as a series of language and literacy events and practices. Researchers use language to engage in their inquiries, to collect and analyze data, to theorize, to reflect, to create knowledge, and to share understandings both with participants and with consumers of their research. And research, no less than any language and literacy event, always involves social relationships, political processes, power relations, and cultural production and reproduction and is always ideological.

By locating discourse analysis within the linguistic turn in the social sciences, we emphasize the centrality of language to social events and to the social construction of everyday life and social institutions such as schooling and education. Although on occasion the social events analyzed may seem small and almost trivial, sometimes at deeper levels such events play critical roles in gatekeeping processes, in defining what it means to be human, in creating opportunities for new meanings and new social relationships, and in adapting extant social structures and resources to address new problems and situations. Framing discourse analysis as part of the linguistic turn in the social sciences also recognizes a broader intellectual and activist agenda extending across disciplines and research perspectives of deconstructing how social relationships and power relations have been constructed—often unjustly—through language and how those relationships might be reconstructed on a more equitable and democratic basis.

LOCAL EVENTS AND THEIR RELATIONSHIPS TO BROADER CULTURAL AND SOCIAL PROCESSES: MICRO LEVEL AND MACRO LEVEL APPROACHES

Micro level approaches to discourse analysis emphasize face-to-face interactions, the immediate situation, and local events. The term *face-to-face* indicates a level of social interaction among people and should not be interpreted as people actually located in the same place or looking at each other. For example, telephone calls, video conferencing, the passing of notes in a classroom, and the exchange of letters or e-mails among specific people, all constitute face-to-face interaction. Macro level approaches emphasize broad social, cultural, and political processes that define social institutions, cultural ideologies, and all that happens within and across them. In our view, it is important to recognize the interplay of discourse processes at both micro and macro levels. As an aside, it is important to note that from a practical perspective it is difficult to conduct a discourse analysis at both micro and macro levels. One level of analysis is usually emphasized over the other. What is at issue, however, is not whether there is a comprehensive discourse analysis at both levels, but rather whether there is recognition of other levels.

One way to conceptualize the relationship of micro level and macro level approaches is shown in Figure 1.1, as if the topics of study in a micro level approach were embedded in macro level processes. Such a model can be helpful in foregrounding the ways

Figure 1.1. Micro level approaches to discourse analysis embedded in macro level approaches.

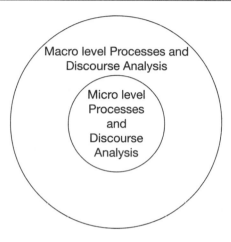

in which macro level processes influence what happens on a face-to-face level. For example, it can foreground broad questions such as the following:

- How are race, class, and gender relations in the broad society reflected in the discourse within a classroom?
- How are the chronotopes (movement through time and space) of grand narratives reflected in literacy events within a classroom discourse?
- How are the goals, tasks, activities, and social relationships constituted through a classroom discourse reflective of the cultural and economic ideologies of the broader society (e.g., individualism, capitalism, social hierarchy, and so on)?
- How are economic structures and processes reflected in and influencing how teachers and students converse with each other, their social relationships, and social identities?

The model represented in Figure 1.1 can also be helpful in fore-grounding societal mechanisms of social control and power relations, such as those identified by Foucault (1965, 1980), as they manifest themselves in a particular classroom discourse. For example, questions such as the following can be asked:

- What mechanisms of surveillance are constituted through classroom discourse?
- What dividing practices are implied within a particular classroom discourse? (Dividing practices refer to the construction of dualisms such as reasonable/unreasonable, sane/insane, good/evil, masculine/feminine, heterosexual/homosexual, educated/uneducated, literate/illiterate, and so on. See Foucault, 1980.)
- Which definitions of knowledge are taken for granted and viewed as common sense and which definitions are viewed as aberrant and irrational? How do these definitions of knowledge privilege some and marginalize others?

In our view, there are at least two ways to approach the model represented in Figure 1.1. What we call the "hard" approach begins with constructs identified in macro level discourse analyses and seeks their iteration at the micro level. The liability of a hard approach is that a researcher may find what she or he is looking for whether such a construct is actually salient within a specific classroom language and literacy event. The researcher may overlook other discourse processes and the ways in which people through their interactions at a face-to-face level resist and reconstruct macro level processes (at least within a local situation or event). A "soft" approach to the model represented in Figure 1.1 generates questions such as those listed above as starting points and as possibilities while the researcher remains open to alternatives, to redefining the starting points, and to abandoning the starting points in favor of local discourse processes that may have more salience in describing and understanding literacy events in the classroom.

An alternative to the model in Figure 1.1 is shown in Figure 1.2, which foregrounds the analysis of micro level discourse processes and incorporates considerations of macro level discourse processes within those micro level analyses. In brief, the model

Figure 1.2. Macro level approaches to discourse analysis embedded in micro level approaches.

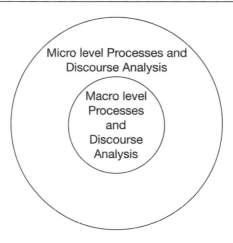

in Figure 1.2 implies that discourse processes at the level of face-to-face events constitute and define macro level processes. For example, questions such as the following might be foregrounded:

- What cultural themes are generated through discoursing at the level of face-to-face interaction within a particular set of classroom literacy events?
- What narratives are generated within and used as interpretive frameworks through the discourse of face-to-face interaction within a particular set of classroom literacy events?
- What interpretive frameworks are constructed through the discourse of face-to-face interaction within a particular set of language and literacy events for interpreting and acting on the world beyond the local event?
- How are power relations defined and constituted among the participants within a particular language and literacy event? How are power relations constituted among participants within a particular event and others outside the event at the level of face-to-face interaction?

One criticism of the model represented in Figure 1.2 is that it underappreciates the influence of macro level discourse processes on local, face-to-face events.

The tension between macro and micro level approaches to discourse analysis reflects acknowledgment that while people live their lives "locally," interacting with others, moving in and out of and across events, they also are influenced by broad social, cultural, political, economic, and historical processes that exist far beyond the local situations in which people interact. After all, we are all born into worlds not of our own making and we must respond to what is already here, even if our response is to resist, to transform, or to create alternatives. People both act upon the worlds in which they live and are acted upon by those worlds.

In our view, discourse analysis studies need to acknowledge both micro level and macro level processes. For example, consider the following literacy event from a first-grade classroom, which is first approached only at a micro level. The transcript begins a few minutes after the first-grade teacher has finished reading *There's an Alligator Under My Bed* (Mayer, 1987) aloud to the students. After reading the story, she put the students into groups of three or four and instructed them to draw a picture of what they had just read. David, Katie, Michelle, and Oscar are in one group, with a large sheet of paper on the floor on which they are drawing:

18 *David:* Are you drawing a house?
19 *Katie:* We need to do this (*she reaches for another crayon*)
20 *Michelle:* Huh / what do you mean? (*spoken in an irritated tone of voice*)
21 *Oscar:* With the alligator
22 ? [undecipherable]
23 *David:* She's drawin' a house (*David looks at the paper then at Oscar and Katie*)
24 *Michelle:* Now I'm gonna …
25 *Oscar:* … I'm gonna do a house, too (*Oscar interrupts Michelle, and looks at Michelle, intonation suggests the statement is a request for permission*)
26 *Katie:* (*moves the crayon box to her left side away from Michelle*)
27 *Michelle:* That's my box (*Michelle reaches for the box*)
28 *Katie:* We need to color

29 *Michelle:* I know (*Katie tries to get a crayon as Michelle takes it. Michelle holds the box close to her body so that no one else can see inside the box.*)

30 *Katie:* I need pink (*David begins drawing again*)

31 *Michelle:* Hold on (*her tone suggests annoyance and anger. Michelle appears to be looking for a pink crayon*)

32 *Michelle:* Don't break that (*Michelle hands Katie the crayon*)

33 *Oscar:* Can I draw a house? (*Oscar sits up on his knees and looks again at Michelle as he poses the question*)

34 *Katie:* Actually I need green/for/there (*Katie looks for green crayon in the box. Oscar sits and looks at Michelle*)

35 *Michelle:* And then I need a window for a marker (*Michelle gets a marker out of the box*)

36 *?:* Hey oh

37 *Michelle:* You can use this marker if you want

38 *Oscar:* I'm gonna / I'm gonna do a house

39 *Katie:* There's other markers

40 *Katie:* How come you had that only marker (*Oscar stares at the picture*)

41 *Katie:* You had more

42 *Michelle:* I know / I put 'em in my desk

43 *Oscar:* I'm / I'm doing a house (*Oscar looks at Michelle. Michelle starts drawing*)

44 *Michelle:* Yea / we don't need a house (*Michelle responds to Oscar without looking up from the paper*)

45 *Katie:* We don't need another house (*Oscar sits still with his pencil in his hand. He is frowning*)

46 *Michelle:* What?

47 *Katie:* We don't need another house

48 *Michelle:* I'm not draw / I'm not drawing another house (Transcript reproduced from Christian & Bloome, 2005)

At the beginning of this transcript, David asks Michelle whether she is drawing a house. The content and function of his question are ambiguous; he might simply be expressing curiosity about what Michelle is drawing, he might want to coordinate the various drawings on the paper so that the key elements from the story are covered, or he might be challenging Michelle's actions in drawing the house perhaps because he wanted to draw the house. His question is ignored by Katie and Oscar (which is a kind of response) and Michelle challenges the meaning of his question and signals that it is a challenge through the tone of her voice. Her response defines David's question in line 18 as a challenge to her drawing the house while simultaneously contesting his right to challenge her. David's appeal to Katie and Oscar (line 23) is ignored. Within these few utterances David is marginalized and silenced in this literacy event. Oscar asks for permission to draw a house (line 25) while Katie attempts to assert control of the crayons (which would enhance her social status and ability to control a resource needed by the others). But Michelle asserts that the box is hers (line 27), takes the box and positions it in a way so that she even controls sight lines to the box (line 29), and positions Katie and the others in subordinate positions so that they must ask her for permission to use a particular color crayon (lines 30 and 31). Although Michelle does give Katie the crayon requested, her giving of the crayon is accompanied by the admonition to not break the crayon (line 32) which can be interpreted as the sort of utterance that an adult might say to a child. Oscar again requests permission to draw a house, this time with an explicit request (line 33), but he is ignored. Katie asks for another color crayon and retrieves it (line 34) uncontested by Michelle, who announces that she needs a marker (line 35). Michelle's public announcement that she needs a marker is not a request for a marker as she controls the crayon and marker box and she does not need anyone's permission to get a marker. Michelle's announcement can be viewed as parallel to Katie's request that she needs a green crayon and potentially is a way of signaling solidarity with Katie. Michelle then extends the use of a marker to Katie (line 37) as if providing her with a privilege; meanwhile Oscar's request to draw a house continues to be ignored even though he announces that he is going to draw a house (line 38). During this time, Michele and Katie continue to draw while talking, but Oscar and David do not draw but look at what Katie and Michelle are drawing. Katie indirectly asks Michelle about the other markers Michelle had (line 40). This can be viewed as an attempt to assign Michelle enhanced social status as Michelle owns a valuable resource, a collection of colored markers. Oscar again asserts that he is going to draw a house (line 43) but he is denied permission to do so (line 44) as Michelle speaks on behalf of the whole group by using the first person plural ("we don't need") and Katie supports Michelle's decision and in so doing signals her solidarity with Michelle (line 45 and 47). Michelle's response is difficult to interpret (line 48, "I'm not draw / I'm not drawing another house"). It could be a misstatement and simply be a reassertion of denial of permission to Oscar to draw a house. It could be that Michelle has misunderstood Oscar's request as asking her to draw another house. Or it could be that Michelle is suggesting to Oscar and the rest of the group that Oscar's drawing skills are so poor that she would have to draw the house for Oscar. It is hard to tell what this utterance is taken to mean as there is no uptake on it by the other children, except that Oscar abandons his request to draw a house (and, we would claim, it is the abandonment of the message that is the meaning of the message). At this point, Katie and Michelle are sitting on the paper drawing, David is sitting on the edge of the paper drawing a very tiny picture, and Oscar is sitting just off of the picture, not drawing, looking at the pictures that Michelle and Katie are drawing. (The procedures used for constructing the analysis of this event can be found in Christian & Bloome, 2005, and in Bloome et al., 2005.)

Based solely on a micro level discourse analysis, one might interpret Michelle as being bossy and controlling. A researcher concerned with how children access opportunities to learn in classroom lessons might view Michelle and Katie as denying Oscar and David such opportunities. Theoretical constructs might be generated that focus on how peer relations constrain learning opportunities with possible implications for how teachers might monitor instructional peer groups and organize instruction.

Layering a macro level discourse analysis to the analysis above can provide additional entry points for analysis and interpretation. For example, consider how the analysis depends on incorporating more macro social theories concerned with race and language (see Dixson & Rousseau, 2005; Goldberg, 1990). The teacher in this classroom is an African American female; Michelle is the only African American female student in the class. Katie is a white female, and the two boys are Latino and English language learners (ELL). A "hard" approach (as described earlier) would look for how the children act out grand narratives of racial and linguistic hierarchy and inequity. Rather than view Michelle as simply a bully, questions might be asked about how a child who is the sole African American student asserts herself as an intellectual and bright student in a predominately white classroom and school in a school district with a history of racial segregation and underserving African American children. What are the racial, cultural, and power relations issues that Michelle must address to academically thrive in that classroom and what are the resources provided for her to do so? Also from a macro level perspective, Katie and Michelle might be viewed as playing out a grand narrative that marginalizes English language learners.

With the limited amount of data provided, no inferences should be made about the teacher and her role in supporting students in her classroom. For the record, it is important to note that we had great esteem for the teacher who worked hard to provide high-quality learning opportunities for all of her students. What is at issue here is not an evaluation of the classroom but an illustration of how research questions, frames, and foci might be generated.

From layering a macro level perspective onto the micro level analysis provided earlier, questions might also be asked about how the children's actions reflect other events in the classroom and how these events as a whole reflect the social significance of race and language within the classroom, the school, and the broader communities in which they live. In this specific setting, classroom instruction and peer conversations are conducted in English only, and David and Oscar are pulled out of the classroom once each day for English as a second language (ESL) instruction. They rarely volunteer to talk during whole-class instruction, and when they do talk their contributions are often askew from the shared cultural and academic knowledge of the other members of the class. Responses by the teacher and by their peers to their rare contributions do not provide them with enhanced social status, but rather just the opposite. The fact that the classroom follows a language policy of English monolingualism is not that of the teacher, the students, personnel in the school, or even the school community, but a legal mandate from the state. The emphasis on English learning by students such as David and Oscar by immersing the children in monolingual English contexts is part of a "common sense" educational ideology of language learning shared by the teacher, the students, the district, and the general public. (What constitutes "common sense" is not necessarily research based nor does it necessarily follow a logical model. See Geertz, 1973.) The inherent positioning of English language learners within such an educational ideology as outsiders who need to work their way into the mainstream is reflected in how David and Oscar are socially marginalized by Michelle and Katie (as well as in their physical marginalization—they sit on the margins of the paper and they are silent in classroom activities). Michelle is a leader and is often recognized by the teacher and other students as knowledgeable and an initiator in other classroom events. Such assertive behavior is consistent with a focus on individual achievement and individual learning that defines assessment and reward practices throughout schooling and beyond. Michelle's achievement and social status can be viewed as contesting the subordinate academic positioning that many African American students and females often suffer in schools, especially when they are a distinct minority in a classroom.

In sum, when viewed at both a micro level and a macro level, what happens in the literacy event related above can be viewed as being constituted by what the students and teacher are doing in interaction with each other and also by a series of events both within and outside of the classroom that connect them to the state, other dominant social institutions, social and cultural ideologies including ideologies about language, race, gender, competition, individualism, and what counts as knowledge within these so-cial institutions. At both the micro level and macro level there is a "common sense" promulgated that naturalizes what is occurring, that makes all of what is occurring appear "reasonable" despite the awkwardness, distress, and pain that close-up micro level dis-course analysis reveals.

Part of the tension between micro level approaches to dis-course analysis and macro level ones is that people in their daily lives may not readily see the machinations of macro level dis-course processes without an explicit focus on such issues. They may not see how classroom literacy events such as the one above differentially socialize students into different kinds of learners and users of spoken and written language. They may not see how such differences are motivated by and feed into social, ra-cial, gendered, and economic stratification in society. Social and cultural processes of control and of establishing "common sense" and "truth" may go unrecognized. Not seeing these macro level processes does not mean that they do not exist or that they do not have material consequence within the ordinary, daily events of people's lives.

Of course, it is not always the case that connections between the micro and macro level discourse processes are not seen. People, including teachers and students, often talk about those relationships (although they may not do so in scholarly terminology). At issue for some educators and researchers is the degree to which making visible the connections between the micro level discourse processes of classroom literacy events and macro level social, cultural, economic, and political processes should be an explicit part of the literacy curriculum. In brief, researchers must be careful not to treat people as if they were merely cultural puppets or embodiments of false consciousness (see Macbeth, 2003). And while it is true that at times it is difficult for people to act upon a situation (as was the case for David and Oscar), at other times people actively and explicitly address the circumstances in which they find themselves, transforming, adapting, resisting, and eschewing those macro level cultural practices in their everyday lives (see Street, 1993b; de Certeau, 1984); and in some cases explicitly undermining them (e.g., see Lasn, 2000, on "culture jamming"). All of these meaning potentials must be considered as part of the framing of a discourse analysis study of language and literacy events in classrooms.

The Importance of Social and Historical Contexts in Discourse Analysis

Regardless of the approach taken or definition of discourse employed, it is our view that discourse and discoursing must be understood as something that exists in contexts. Despite widespread agreement that capturing context is important, there has been ongoing debate about how to define, explore, and describe *context*. In part, the debate reflects differences across disciplines: Psychologists focus on the context of psychological processes of the individual; sociologists on the context of social and political structures; historians focus on the historical context of particular events, and so on. Even if one tried to capture all of these contexts, one would never be able to capture the entire context. But more importantly, attempting to do so misses the point: *Context* is not a set of independent variables that influence an event, but a set of socially constructed relationships among one event and other events, among people in one place and people in other places, between one social institution and another social institution, between one time and other times, and so on. And these relationships are "motivated," that is, they are as much about the construction of meaning, power relations, identities, and social relationships as they are reflections of them. Thus the debate over context is partly about how we understand these constructions.

The debate is also about definitions of *culture*. Differences in how to define culture have evolved as anthropologists and others have tried to capture the social behavior of people in the full complexity and continuous change of their daily lives. Some ways that culture has been defined include as customs, habits, and norms (e.g., Tylor, 1871/1958); as shared standards and expectations for acting, believing, feeling, valuing, speaking, and thinking (e.g., Goodenough, 1981); as a set of shared models for understanding events, actions, people, and oneself (e.g., Holland & Quinn, 1987); and as "webs of significance" created by people and within which people act (Geertz, 1973). More recently, the concept of culture itself has been criticized, and some have argued that the concept and term should be abandoned because of its "neocolonial, racist and nationalist overtones" (Heath & Street, 2008, p. 7). One approach to defining culture that provides the flexibility to capture the complexity of people's lives is to define culture as a verb (Street, 1993a; Heath & Street, 2008). From the perspective of culture as a verb, one does not ask what culture is, but what culture does. Since we view that perspective as having important implications for understanding context in discourse analysis studies of language and literacy events in classrooms, we quote at length from Heath and Street's (2008) discussion of the implications of defining culture as a verb:

> Social constructivists and some anthropologists (including Brian [Street] and Shirley [Heath]) pushed hard for the idea that culture never just "is," but instead "does" (Thornton, 1988, p. 26). Street (1993) proposed that we think of culture as a verb rather than as a noun—a fixed thing. Ethnographers who adopted this idea took culture to be unbounded, kaleidoscopic, and dynamic. In their studies of ever-shifting active processes of meaning-making in situations, ethnographers search for interconnected patterns (see Shuman, 1986, for an illustration of this principle in a study of secondary students in and out of school). In their focused observation and participation within a chosen physical location or

an identifiable social group, ethnographers adopting the culture-as-verb idea take as axiomatic the following principles as they think ahead to their field studies of language and multimodal literacies.

1. Gradations of change in habits and beliefs (though seemingly minor on the *surface*) correlate with shifts in structures and uses of language and multimodal literacies.

2. Singular or "essential" meanings or explanations that come in authoritative or institutionally grounded terms must be open to scrutiny in *historical* and operational frames.

3. The same goes for discourse forms and illustrative materials that stick out or are formalized, authorized, named, and valorized (especially through state-sanctioned and -supported institutions or commercial interests).

4. Insiders or locals use *tacit meaning-making processes* that they take for granted, and their explanations of these often bear little relationship to realities of usage. They may be expressing ideals of behavior rather than *manifest, or actual, behavior.*

5. The norm in (almost) all contexts is that we coordinate the regularities of patterns of *several systems of symbolic structure* at the same time. (pp. 7–8, emphases added)

The principles listed by Heath and Street provide guidance in constructing what is sometimes called the "ethnographic context." Although an ethnographic study may not accompany every discourse analysis study, the discourse analysis of a social event needs to be predicated on acknowledgment that it exists within an ethnographic context.

Defining where and when an event takes place is a multilayered task. Locating a literacy event within a classroom is not enough. It may occur during "free reading time," which varies from reading that takes place during an instructional reading group or a whole-class choral reading. Even though the focus may be on the same content or written text, the way in which the group engages with that content may vary depending upon their various histories and their relationship with reading and writing. The context of the literacy event differs if the participants are Robin, Valerie, Michael, Stephen, and Ms. Smith or if the group also includes Mark, who is Robin's twin, or the student teacher from the elite, predominantly white university across town. And it makes a difference if the students come from communities and families that are middle-class, working-class, white, African American, Latino, or heterogeneously diverse. It makes a difference whether the classroom is in a school district and state that has adopted federal mandates for reading education or one that has resisted such mandates. The particularities of the school, the communities, the families, the social institutions, the natural environment—what makes each unique—matter. And while one cannot and should not predict what difference each of these and other contextual aspects makes a priori, in the history of education in the United States and many other places such contextual aspects are often part of how people assign meaning to what they and others are doing.

Earlier in this chapter we presented a view of context represented by concentric circles (Figures 1.1 and 1.2). Although such a view of context may be a helpful beginning, a model of context as concentric circles of broader and broader contexts is inadequate for understanding how people locate the social events in which they are participating. In order to demonstrate that a more complex model of context is needed, we shall now consider the literacy event transcribed below that comes from a first-grade classroom.

The teacher announces that it is time for reading group and the students leave their desks and go to the "reading carpet." When they get to the carpet, the teacher distributes copies of the book they have been reading, a leveled reader entitled *Mortimer Frog* (Cullinan, 1989). The story is about a teacher and her students who have a frog named Mortimer in their classroom. Mortimer is growing and they are trying to decide if they should get Mortimer a new tank. The children are seated on the carpet and all of them are holding a copy of the reader. The teacher is sitting on a chair in front of the students with a copy of *Mortimer Frog* in her hands. This transcript begins with a choral reading of a sentence printed in the book.

101 *Teacher and Students:* "'Do you think Mortimer wants a new tank?' asked Ms. Lee." (*choral reading, some students "mouth" words while watching other students and others read aloud while looking at the book.*)

102 *Carl:* If y'all want a new . . . um . . . tank for Ms. . . .

103 *Teacher:* They said . . . do you think Mortimer wants a new tank?

104 *Carl:* They keep (*pause*) puttin' him in . . .

105 *Teacher:* Do you think they want a new tank?

106 *Students:* No.
107 *Teacher:* Let's read it to yourselves
108 (*Students lower heads and immediately put their finger on the page to track the words*)
109 And see if Mortimer needs a new tank.
110 Read it to yourself.
111 OK.
112 Raise your hand.
113 Katherine, what . . .
114 I mean Katie.
115 What did his . . . what did Todd say that . . . that Mortimer likes to do?
116 OK. Oscar.
117 *Oscar:* To take big steps.
118 *Teacher:* To take big hops. Yes.
119 He likes to take big hops.
120 And is the . . . is the tank a good place for him?
121 *Students:* No.
122 *Students:* Yes.
123 *Teacher:* Are you sure?
124 *Students:* No
125 *Teacher:* Who can find me a sentence that says the tank is not a good place for him?
126 Who can read the sentence . . .
127 The sentence will be on page 35.
128 Who can tell . . . who can say that the . . .
129 That he likes to take big hops
130 I mean that the tank isn't good for him.
131 Look in your book.
132 Look in your book.
133 Who can find the sentence that says that the tank isn't good for 'im?
134 You need to read it
135 Don't fake it.
136 You need to read it.

In a discourse analysis of this event, one might examine aspects that occur even before the first utterance. A decision was made by the textbook publisher to include a story about a frog and a boy in a reader intended for first-grade children. A corresponding decision was made by personnel in the school district to purchase that reader as appropriate for first-grade children and a decision was made by the teacher to use that story in the reading lesson. These decisions reflect shared expectations about what interests children of that age. But the interests of first-grade children are not given by their age but derive from cultures of childhood. There is not a single culture of childhood for all children; there are cultures of childhood that vary across cultural groups, as well as across gender and other dimensions. Thus the decisions made about readings that interest first-grade children are as much projective as they are reflective. These decisions and the way they constitute a culture of childhood are part of the cultural, social, and historical context of this classroom language and literacy event.

This literacy event begins with a choral reading of the text. This is a reading practice that the teacher and students have used frequently before in similar circumstances. The children know the shared expectations for how to do a choral reading, the cadence expected, the volume, how to follow the teacher's lead, how to show that they are appropriately participating through display of eye gaze and moving their mouths. Their choral reading practices are related to their past choral reading events. But it is also related to pedagogical suggestions provided in the teacher's manual, and those suggestions are related to advice derived by people working for the publisher from articles in professional journals written by university scholars. It is the same for the other reading practices found in this event: the use of a finger to guide the students' silent reading (line 108), the asking of comprehension questions at both literal and interpretive levels (lines 105, 115, 120) with an emphasis on answers supported by textual evidence (lines 125, 131, 132, 133, 134, 136). The requirement that responses be supported by textual evidence is related to the goal of learning how to construct an academic argument with claims, warrants, and evidence—a goal that looks forward to the kinds of academic demands that will be made of the students in later grades. In terms of context, therefore, this event is linked with past and future events in the classroom, with contexts of policy decisions regarding reading curriculum made by district and state administrators, with decisions made by publishers involving both the pedagogical nature of their texts and manuals as well as marketing aspects, with contexts of reading research at universities, and with the curriculum of future academic subject areas.

The classroom event is also contextualized by the need for students to orient to the ongoing assessment of their reading and classroom behavior by the teacher (and by each other). Mostly the assessment and surveillance go unstated and are invisible. It is only when there is a breakdown in the required behavior that the assessment and surveillance become visible. In line 135 the teacher admonishes the students, "Don't fake it." Some of the students have been only mouthing the words (line 101). Although they may indeed be mouthing the printed words and perhaps thinking about the meanings of the printed words, alternatively they may be engaged in mock participation (cf. Bloome, Puro, & Theodorou, 1987). When the teacher asks the students a question pertaining to what they have read—"What'd Ms. Lee ask the children?"—many students do not respond. In brief, one set of contexts of this event concerns shared expectations for how to "do schooling" and for the obligations of teachers and students toward each other and toward the assessment system.

The questioning initiated by the teacher derives in part from the teacher's manual, but it also derives from patterns of questioning that have permeated classroom instruction broadly and for at least a half century. This pattern of questioning is often described as the asking of known-information questions or as Initiation-Response-Evaluation/Feedback (IRE) sequences. The teacher initiates an inquiry (usually through asking a questions), the student responds, and the teacher provides feedback on the response usually in the form of an evaluation. For example, in the classroom literacy event above, the teacher asks, ". . . what did Todd say that . . . that Mortimer likes to do?"(line 115) and Oscar responds, "To take big steps" (line 117). The teacher repeats Oscar's answer changing *steps* to *hops* (line 118), indicates it is the correct answer by saying "Yes" (line 118), and then rephrases his answer as a complete sentence, a type of feedback (line 119), making the evaluation and feedback public to the class. The questioning pattern and the way in which the questioning pattern locates authority in the teacher for correct knowledge and for what counts as knowledge is also a context of the event. Such a context might be labeled an institutional context as the questioning pattern is a marker of an institutional discourse almost exclusively associated with schools.

This discussion of the event restated above and the many different kinds of contexts in which it is located indeed shows that a view of context as concentric circles (as shown in Figures 1.1 and 1.2) is too simplistic for broader contexts. Context needs to be understood as historical (relating both to past and future events), multiple (including potentially contradictory and contesting contexts), at multiple levels, and as interactive (contexts affect each other). Building on Bakhtin's (1935/1981, 1953/1986) and Volosinov's (1929/1973) discussions of language, we assert that every utterance, every word, every response, every use of language, every prosodic and nonverbal behavior brings with it a history of uses, connotations, connections, implications, nuances, frames, footings, social relationships, identities, constraints, and possibilities. As people interact with each other and create or re-create social events, they locate uses of spoken and written language and related semiotic systems within a community or social institution, like school, and within a history (or histories) that are both their own and those of others (such as their families', their communities', the institution's, and so on). Thus to emphasize context is to emphasize that every language and literacy event has productive relationships with other events and social institutions (such as schooling). The model of discourse analysis shown in Figure 1.3 foregrounds the understanding that there are always multiple contexts at play at any one time, and that an event itself is also a context.

Contexts and events are related to each other historically, both to what has occurred before and to what will occur in the future (as indicated by the arrows in Figure 1.3). Contexts and events are also related to simultaneously occurring contexts and events; and all of these contexts and events seep into each other, they are not distinct or isolatable.

DISCOURSE PROCESSES AND POWER RELATIONS

We need to begin this section with a caveat. Although discourse processes always involve power relations, not every discourse analysis study examines power relations or needs to do so. Power relations are not always the salient issue in language and literacy events and the social relationships that people create are not necessarily defined by power. Although power relations are important

Figure 1.3. Events and contexts in historical and multiple relationships.

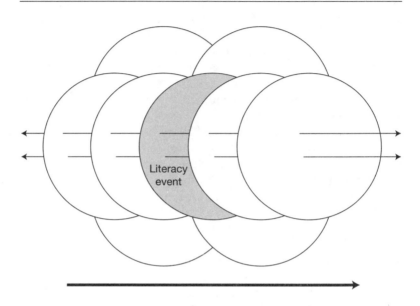

to examine, it is also important to examine caring relations, solidarity and unity among people, the mutual extension of dignity and respect, and the way that people often background power hierarchies as they create meaningful lives for themselves, their families, and their communities.

For heuristic purposes, *power* can be defined as product and as process. Power as product refers to those definitions of power in which a person, group, institution, or other social entity imposes itself by strength of force. Some examples include larger armies, more destructive weapons, more money, and so on. Power as product also refers to equations of power and skills; more reading and writing skills, more education, a more extensive social network, more cultural capital, and a larger vocabulary all equal more power. Similarly, power as product can refer to equations of power and opportunity: The more opportunities and access one has to a society's rewards, tools, and resources, the more power one has.

Definitions of power as process foreground the situated nature of power relations among people and among institutions. The larger army does not always prevail, the person with more writing skills does not always compose the most compelling story, and the teacher does not always control what happens in classrooms—sometimes the students do (see Candela, 1999). People find ways to adapt imposed cultural forms to other agendas (e.g., Kulik & Stroud, 1993), undermine authoritarian discourse with parody (see Bakhtin, 1935/1981), create spaces for agency (see De Certeau, 1984), and otherwise complicate and problematize simple and decontextualized equations of quantity and power. The particular social contours of a particular situation frame the power relations among participants and among social institutions.

For example, consider the various grand narratives associated with reading and literacy. Children are taught to read, and having learned to read, do well in school and then find good jobs to support a good life. Children who are not taught to read and who do not learn to read are liable to fail in school, fail to find a good job, and fail to have a good life. Such a grand narrative appears to make it a moral imperative to extend the teaching of reading to every child and to insist that they learn to read. It sets up a dividing practice (see Foucault, 1980) between those who read and those who do not and between those who support the teaching of reading to all children and those who do not. Those who support the teaching of reading to all children have common sense, are rational, and are morally righteous; those who oppose such efforts lack common sense, are irrational, and are morally bankrupt. Yet, as anthropologists, ethnographers, critical discourse analysts, educational researchers, and other scholars have shown, there are many ways of reading and many ways of learning to read. Reading is not a monolithic, autonomous process, but a diverse set of social practices involving written language. For example, in his study of literacy in Iranian villages, Street (1993b) showed how the government took on the grand narratives of reading described earlier. They sent teachers trained in the teaching of reading from the cities to the villages to teach the villagers to read. But the government and its teachers overlooked the reading and literacy practices the villagers already had, including the reading the villagers did for religious purposes and for their businesses.

The teachers created a situation that was dysfunctional for many of the young people taught at the government schools. They ended up fitting neither with their village nor with the cities from which the teachers had come. In brief, what looked like common sense was instead an exercise of power that disadvantaged those already marginalized. The power is in what the framing is and how a particular framing is made hegemonic.

We want to end this chapter with a reminder that the research enterprise itself also exists in a context. The issues described above about contextualizing language and literacy events in classrooms apply also to research enterprises including discourse analysis studies. They are no less historical, cultural, political, and ideological; and they no less involve power relations. While it is rarely practical for researchers to conduct an ethnographic study of the research enterprise while also conducting the research, nonetheless, researchers should be reflexively aware of the contexts of their research and take that into account with regard to how they interact with and affect people and events, what descriptions they create, and how their research is used by themselves and others.

CHAPTER 2

Discourse as a Noun and
Discourse as a Verb

For readers of discourse analysis studies and scholars interested in conducting discourse analysis, it is crucial to have a sense of available approaches and perspectives and their traditions of use in educational research (Rex & Green, 2008). There are several useful books that list different approaches to discourse analysis and provide a brief description of each approach (see Supplemental Bibliographies). In this chapter we take a different approach. In our view, it is important to have an understanding of the ways that discourse has been defined because that frames the analysis conducted. Each definition of discourse can be viewed as providing a different set of perspectives, affordances, constraints, and potential research problems and questions; each definition is a different way to redefine extant concepts of language and literacy events in classrooms.

Among others, McHoul (2001) has also noted the diverse ways in which *discourse* has been defined, but goes further by framing definitions of "discourse" by the type of noun researchers have taken discourse to be.

> 'Discourse,' used as a mass noun, means roughly the same as 'language *use*' or 'language-*in-use*.' As a count noun ('a discourse') it means a relatively discrete subset of a whole language, used for specific social or institutional purposes—as in 'the medical discourses of the middle ages.' Occasionally the 'count' usage becomes 'massified' —as in 'Aristotelian scientific discourse' or (and therefore ambiguously) 'the discourse on childhood.' The second usage carries the implication that discourse is a way of

ordering categories of thought and knowledge, echoing the 'ordinary' meaning of 'a discourse' as a kind of text or treatise. In
some critical branches of philosophy and semiotics, the term
'discursive' carries with it the sense of 'textually or linguistically
produced.' Thus madness, for example, may be referred to as
'discursively constructed,' to show that it does not exist as a 'real
fact' in the world but is fabricated within certain forms of knowledge or 'disciplines,' often for particular political purposes. (pp.
133–134, emphasis in original)

Like McHoul, we came across many research studies that
used discourse as a noun. On occasion we found uses of discourse
as a personified and animated noun, as if it had agency of its own,
as in "The discourse positioned the student as marginalized" (see
Bloome & Clark, 2006, for additional discussion of the animation
of discourse). Sometimes, as the subject of a sentence, discourse
is paired with the verb *is*, as in "Discourse is socially constituted"
(Wodak, 1996, p. 15, quoted in Titscher et al., 2000, p. 26). Pairing
discourse with *is* creates the effect of viewing discourse as if the
characteristic ascribed to discourse is something integral to it or a
"truth," rather than a characteristic ascribed to it by people.

Although it is rare, we also found that discourse has been used
as a verb. Van Dijk (1997) lists "Discourse as action and interaction
in society" (p. 13) as one of several definitions of discourse. *The
Compact Edition of the Oxford English Dictionary* (1971, p. 745) provides a historical definition of discourse as a verb, as in the Latin
"*discurrere* to run to and fro . . . to run, travel or move over a space
. . . to turn over in the mind . . . to think about . . . to speak or converse with (a person), to talk to." In a volume edited by Norris
and Jones (2005), *discourse* is defined as a set of actions taken with
and through language that mediate social interactions and social
events. Defining discourse as a verb is reminiscent of Street's definition of culture as a verb (1993a; see also Heath & Street, 2008; see
Chapter 1 for a full discussion of culture as a verb) in that the focus
is shifted from what discourse *is* to what discourse *does*. It is also
reminiscent of Tracy's (1995) discussion of action-implicative discourse analysis. She argues that focusing on conversational action
as rhetorical (including the rhetorics of how actors have framed a
situation's problems) implies a different logic-of-inquiry, one that
focuses on what people do (their interactions and uses of language)
and their reflections and discoursing on their actions and events.

We found the use of discourse as a verb appealing because it resonates with our experiences when engaged in the discourse analysis of language and literacy events in classrooms, because it foregrounds how people *act on* and *interact with* the complex, confounded, indeterminate, and meandering meanings, significances, and consequences of an event, social practice, or text.

In the sections that follow, we first discuss discourse as a noun and then as a verb. We organize this discussion of definitions of discourse as one way to "map" the variations in definitions of discourse and approaches to discourse analysis. There are other ways to categorize definitions of discourse: for example, by discipline, by focus on text versus conversation, by attending to micro sociological processes such as face-to-face interaction versus macro sociological processes such as the political ideologies of nation-states (as discussed in Chapter 1). Each way of categorizing definitions of discourse foregrounds one set of insights and backgrounds others.

DISCOURSE AS A NOUN

In this section, we discuss implications of defining discourse as a noun for researching language and literacy events in classrooms. Consider grammatical constructions such as

- classroom discourse
- the discourse of schooling
- "the discourse of the state"
- "mathematical discourse"
- "pedagogical discourse"
- "conversational discourse"
- "achievement discourse" (Bechely, 1999)
- "integration discourse" (Bechely, 1999)
- "constitutive units of discourse"(Galasinski, 2000)
- "cyberspace discourse" (Punday, 2000)
- "the ways that meaning is expressed through discourse" (Mishler, 1986)
- a literate discourse
- the discourse of business penetrates the discourse of schooling

- "discourse is studied within its global and local context" (Galasinski, 2000)
- "a discourse is a sort of identity kit" (Gee, 1996)

As a noun, discourse is sometimes placed in the objective case and treated as an object or concept that can be acquired or as an object of study, as in "The students were acquiring a literate discourse." Alternatively, discourse is sometimes used in the subject position—"The discourse penetrates . . ." or "The discourse captures. . . ." When used as a subject position, discourse itself appears to be animated and have agency, as in "A discourse produces identity through the roles and positions it makes possible."

Below we discuss four definitions of discourse as a noun:

- Discourse as text
- Discourse as language-in-use
- Discourse as identity
- Discourse as truth, rationality, and common sense

These are not the only definitions of discourse as a noun, but they do provide a range of definitions that allow us to address key issues in the reading and conduct of discourse analysis studies of language and literacy events in classrooms. After discussing each of these four definitions of discourse as a noun, we pull them together as a way to redefine literacy curriculum.

Discourse as Text

As text, discourse can be defined simply as words on paper or as a stretch of spoken words (and similar manifestations of language including pictures, graphics, and so on) that are taken as a whole, that is considered a unit. Under the label of *discourse analysis,* researchers may conduct what is also called *textual analysis,* the analysis of those cognitive, linguistic, or political processes that make a unit of language cohere and have meaning (for further discussion of this perspective on discourse analysis, see Widdowson, 2004).

However, as Titscher et al. (2000) point out, defining *text* is more difficult than it might at first seem. What we would ordinarily think of as a text (e.g., a printed page) might be viewed as a text artifact rather than a text itself (see Silverstein & Urban, 1996). From such a perspective, text is a social space in which people create meaning. In other words, a printed text is an artifact of the process of textualization (Bloome & Egan-Robertson, 1993), the transformation by people of events, experiences, or any phenomenon into language. Silverstein and Urban (1996) call this process "entextualization" to emphasize the incorporation of historical processes that contribute to the construction of the text. Such definitions of a text are similar to Volosinov's (1929/1973) philosophy of language which we discussed in the introduction. Each utterance and word, each text, brings with it the meanings and contexts of its previous uses, both reflecting them and refracting them as the text addresses the future.

But what distinguishes a text from a word or utterance? What distinguishes one text from another? Is a basal reader with its series of stories and reading exercises one text or multiple texts? If it is one text because all of the pages are bound together within one cover, does it become multiple texts if the stories and reading exercises are published separately? Such questions are not pedantic; they seek to understand what is the unit of analysis in discourse analysis studies of text(s). How the unit of analysis is defined reflects underlying theoretical assumptions about how texts mean and thus how one might engage in discourse analysis.

Bloome et al. (2005) provide one approach to defining the boundaries of a text. They argue that boundaries are useful meaning-making tools that people in interaction with each other use to signal their meanings. Similar to studies of stories in ethnomethodology (e.g., Jefferson, 1978), Bloome et al. argue that people must signal the beginning of a text and its end. For example, consider the transcript below in which a seventh-grade teacher tells a story in order to illustrate the topic of the class's instructional conversation. They are having a conversation about language variation, race, code switching, and proper and improper language.

201 *Teacher:* OK
202 <u>What</u> is proper and <u>what</u> is slang ↑
203 *Help me out*
204 let me give you a small story
205 You guys

206 where was I born ↑
207 You guys know this.
208 *Camika:* California ↑
209 *Teacher:* <u>no</u>
210 *Janet:*   ⌐ New York
211 *Student:* | Chicago.
212 *Student:* ⌐ I dunno.
213 *Teacher:* I was born in New York and moved to
      California.
214 *Theresa*: Yea that's where you grew up.
215 *Teacher:* When I moved to California I was teased when I
      was little because people told me I talked white
216 How many of your ever heard that phrase *you sound
      white* ↑
217 *Students:* XXXXXXXXXX (*many students talk at once and
      raise hands*)
218 Teacher: Now how come white people never hear that
      phrase *you sound white* ↑
(For a full list of transcription symbols, see Figure 3.2 in
      Chapter 3.)

In line 204 the teacher announces that she is going to tell a
story. The text of the story has not yet begun. By announcing that
she is going to tell a story she is announcing a new pattern for
taking turns at talk. Instead of the back-and-forth of classroom
recitation, she will be taking a series of turns at talk in a row so
that she can tell her story. She is also signaling to the students that
they need to interpret what is coming up as a single text with a
beginning, middle, and end. The text of the story is embedded in
the instructional conversation, but the students should treat the
story as a unit of analysis.

There is no pause or wait for ratification from the students
after announcing that she was going to tell a story in line 204. The
teacher immediately asks a question oriented to the beginning of
her story (line 206 "Where was I born?"). The story actually begins
on line 213. Although not represented in the transcript, there is a
shift in the prosodic contour when the teacher utters line 213. It is
a deviation from the conversational pattern of question-answer-
feedback that preceded line 213 and that dominated most of the
lesson. The utterance itself is not a request for response; indeed,

it assumes that there will be no response. (Line 214 uttered by Theresa is a side comment and not part of the turn taking per se). Line 215 continues the story. Line 216 marks the end of the story by returning to the pattern of question-answer-feedback and to the prosodic contours that preceded the story. In brief, the teacher marks the text of the story as:

> I was born in New York and moved to California. When I moved to California I was teased when I was little because people told me I talked white.

What Bloome et al. (2005) argue is that what constitutes a text, what its boundaries are, cannot be determined until the text is in use. Once the boundaries of a text are identified, then questions can be asked about the contexts within which the text is embedded. As suggested in Chapter 1, people do signal to each other how they are contextualizing their words, utterances, and texts. And they do so at both a micro and macro level.

Of course, the words of the text are also important to its interpretation. They carry meaning and their collective structure shape the story. There are a number of cohesive devices in the story above: the repetition of lexical items and phrases such as "moved to California," syntactic structures that connect clauses using conjunctions like "because," and the sequencing of events through the use of "when." Yet, the words, cohesive devices, and sequential structuring only take on importance and contribute to interpretation within the context of use and in relation to other texts (such as the text of the instructional conversation) and contexts (such as the context of schooling). Fairclough (1992, 2003) argues that texts should be considered within the context of production and the context of consumption. Consider a curriculum document: Questions would be asked about the context of its production (Who was involved? What were their purposes including the implicit social, cultural, and political purposes? What social, cultural, economic, and political ideologies frame the production of the text? And so on.) as well as the context of its consumption (Who are the consumers? How is it used? What social, cultural, and political role does the text play? How does the text assert a particular set of meanings within the context of its consumption and marginalize other meanings? How does the text frame power relations among the people within the context of consumption? And so on.) In brief, the interpretation of a text depends on the text itself, the boundaries of the text, and how the text relates to and is embedded in various contexts.

One approach to discourse as text is critical discourse analysis. Although for the purpose of brevity we treat critical discourse analysis below as if it were a monolithic perspective, in fact there are many different approaches (see Blommaert & Bulcaen, 2000; Rogers, 2004). From the perspective of critical discourse analysis, texts always contribute to the structuring of power relations at both the micro and macro levels (e.g., Fairclough, 1989, 1992, 1995, 2003; Gee, 1996; Ivanic, 1998; Lewis, 2001; Luke, 1996; Rogers, 2004; Wodak, 1996). Texts do so in part because of how they represent people and events, by what they foreground and background, by what they include and exclude, and by how they promulgate a way of understanding the world as natural and common sense (with other ways of understanding the world positioned as deviant and irrational if they are acknowledged at all).

Close attention is paid in critical discourse analysis to the linguistic means by which texts accomplish the structuring of power relations, including a focus on nominalizations (turning processes into nouns), the metaphors used, passive constructions, the use of transitive and intransitive verbs, the use of the present tense of the verb *to be*, and who is framed as an actor and who as acted upon.

One focus of critical discourse analysis studies is how particular ways of acting, thinking, valuing, feeling, structuring and organizing social relationships are produced and taken to be "natural" and "common sense." What counts as knowledge, what counts as truth, what count as morality, what counts as sanity are all mechanisms for producing social order and social life. When such things are "natural" and "common sense," the power they exert in controlling people is invisible and unquestioned.

Discourse as Language-in-Use

Discourse as language-in-use refers to how people use language within the complex give-and-take of the interactions and events that make up their lives. Considered broadly, language-in-use includes all of the semiotic devices that might be used in a face-to-face interaction such as utterances, prosody, nonverbal actions, pictures, and the use of artifacts and objects.

Although researchers focusing on language-in-use must attend not only to the creative and particular aspects of language-in-use but also to the structural, shared, and given aspects, researchers vary in what they emphasize. Some researchers emphasize the creative and particularistic aspects of language-in-use, asking what makes the use of language in a particular event different from the use of language in a similar type of event and, more important, what implications these creative and particularistic uses of language have for the people involved (see Becker, 1988; Bloome & Bailey, 1992). Researchers concerned with the creative and particularistic uses of language are often interested in how people in interaction with each other transform events, identities, and institutions and how they change the social relationships among themselves and between themselves and others. Other researchers focusing on language-in-use emphasize the social and linguistic *practices* of a group such as a disciplinary field, a profession, a social institution, a cultural group, or a classroom; that is, the ways they use language. From this emphasis, when one asks about the discourse of schooling, for example, one is asking about the social and linguistic practices that constitute schooling, that give it meaning and give its "inhabitants" identities and standards for acting, believing, perceiving, talking, and valuing (cf. Goodenough's, 1981, definition of culture).

The conception of discourse as a set of social practices for doing schooling and doing school reading shifts the definition of reading from a set of autonomous cognitive skills (a taken-for-granted definition of reading in most schools that has been critiqued by Street, 1984, 1995, among others) to a definition of reading that makes reading itself a social practice defined both by the social institution in which it is embedded and by the specific situation and event in which it occurs. For example, "doing" reading group is a shared social practice within a classroom and across classrooms. Children learn how to "do" reading group, even if the enactment of a specific reading group on a specific day varies in the story read, the questions asked, and the people present. Although the location, text, and children might be different, the practice of doing reading group will be similar. Classrooms are often built and arranged to support a particular set of reading and literacy practices. For example, there may be an alcove with a table and six to eight chairs to accommodate doing reading group. Instructional programs may be designed around the use of reading groups and administrators may demand their use and hold teachers and students accountable for enacting them.

For researchers emphasizing creativity and particularity, an emphasis would be placed on examining a specific reading group event and the ways in which the teacher and students use language in that event to create social relationships and meaning specific to them. Attention would be placed on how they transformed the event so that it was more than just a replication of past reading group events in their classroom or on how they failed to do so. As we hope is clear from the discussion above, regardless of whether one is emphasizing creativity and particularity or the recurrences of language and literacy practices, researchers concerned with the analysis of language-in-use must attend to both. Further, the analysis of language-in-use, regardless of emphasis, must entail more than a narrow description of linguistic forms or strategies, but rather must extend to help create a contextualized understanding of how language is used to "do social work" whether that social work is creating social relationships; establishing or assigning social identities; structuring relations of power; dividing labor; distributing rewards, resources, and privileges; or just passing through time.

Discourse as Identity

One way to define *identity* or social identity is as a role or position that one assumes or is assigned within a social group or network. Indeed, assuming or being assigned a role implies an affiliation with that social group or network, and that affiliation is part of one's identity. A discourse produces identity through the roles and positions it makes possible, the tools and mechanisms it provides for people to use in assuming and assigning themselves and others to various roles and positions, and in the boundaries it creates between insiders (members of the social group or network) and outsiders (Blackburn, 2005).

For example, in the case of classroom reading groups, assignment to a particular reading group provides a student with a particular "reading" identity (they are a member of a particular group). When reading groups are organized by reading ability, their "reading" identities are organized along an ability scale—high, average, and low. Students who are assigned to the robins, for example, not only have an identity as "robins" but also as high-level readers, a status above those students who are cardinals and have identities as low-level readers. These identities may be limited to reading instruction time or to academics, but there is some evidence that these identities cross over into other activities, including nonacademic ones (Bossert, 1979). Some scholars have argued that the practice of using reading groups and sorting students into high, average, and low reading ability groups derives from the discourse of American reading pedagogy, itself a derivative of the political and social discourse of meritocracy (Borko & Eisenhart, 1987; Eder, 1981; Hiebert, 1983; McDermott, 1977; Slavin, 1993).

But the dynamics of discourse and identity are not just matters of group affiliation, label, and rank. Gee (1996) defines *Discourses* as various "ways of being in the world," as "ways of behaving, interacting, valuing, thinking, believing, speaking, and often reading and writing" (p. viii). Gee distinguishes between discourse with a lowercase "d" and Discourse with an uppercase "D." The lowercase discourse refers to ways of using language within a specific event (the micro level) while the uppercase Discourse refers to "ways of being in the world" (1996, p. viii) (the macro level). Participation in a particular Discourse requires one to be a certain type of person, to assume a particular identity. Each of the reading groups in the example above may have their own ways of using language, their own Discourse (cf. Borko & Eisenhart, 1989). Across the groups, the teacher may ask students to engage the reading text in different ways, ask different kinds of questions, expect different kinds of responses, and hold students accountable for interacting, valuing, and believing in particular ways distinct from the other reading groups. Students within a particular reading group may learn the ways of using language associated with their reading group (the Discourse) and thus their identity as a robin, bluebird, or cardinal is not just an interchangeable identity nor just an indicator of reading rank, but also a marker of a particular "culture" (or subculture) to which they belong (see Borko & Eisenhart, 1989). As such, self-fulfilling prophecies may begin to be constructed as children who view themselves as a member of a particular reading culture embody the discourse appropriate (despite their actual and potential ability) to that group, which further reinforces the child's sense of belonging in that reading group, as well as the teacher's and other students' assumptions about the child's identity and location as a reader.

One of the dynamics regarding discourse and identity concerns who is allowed to have a particular identity. That is, although a Discourse may provide a set of differentiated identities for people affiliated with the group, others are not even allowed to affiliate and thus are assigned the identity of outsider. Labels such as *citizen* and *alien, believer* and *nonbeliever, normal* and *deviant, civilized* and *uncivilized, rational* and *irrational, legal* and *illegal,* all index Discourses that create boundaries between insiders and outsiders. A particular curriculum can influence and restrict the social identities available (see Wortham, 2006). The ways in which Discourses create insiders and outsiders can be subtle (though nonetheless powerful) and not necessarily obvious in extant labels. For example, Gee (1996) argues that differences between a person's "primary Discourse" and the "secondary Discourse" of a social institution, such as school, can create identities aligned with insiders and outsiders, even if those labels are not used.

> [Primary Discourses are] those to which people are apprenticed early in life during their primary socialization as members of particular families within their sociocultural settings. Primary Discourses constitute our first social identity, and something of a base within which we acquire or resist later Discourses. They form our initial taken-for-granted understandings of who we are and who people "like us" are, as well as what sorts of things we ("people like us") do, value, and believe when we are not "in public.". . . Secondary Discourses are those to which people are apprenticed as part of their socializations within various local, state, and national groups and institutions outside early home and peer-group socialization—for example, churches, gangs, schools, and offices. They constitute the recognizability and meaningfulness of our "public" (more formal) acts. (p. 137).

When the Discourse of a social institution such as a school conflicts with a person's primary Discourse, then those people may be at risk of being positioned as different, inferior, or "other." They may have to choose between the identity associated with their primary Discourse and the identity associated with the secondary Discourse of the school or other dominant social institution.

Whether one agrees with Gee's conception of primary and secondary Discourses (see Delpit & Kilgour-Dowdy, 2002, for a different perspective), and whether one agrees that schools force students to choose between the identity associated with school discourse or their home Discourse or culture, clearly there are identity issues related to language and literacy practices in classrooms. These are not surface level matters of labels, but involve deep processes for who can use language, and how, when, where, with whom, and for what purpose. Identity issues do not stand outside of the power relationships embedded within the discourse of a reading group, a classroom, or any other social institutional setting. The identity one assumes or is assigned is aligned with a set of privileges, responsibilities, and obligations; and the positive and negative consequences that result from acting on these privileges, responsibilities, and obligations are made "common sense" by the discourse of the social group and social institution. More simply stated, not responding to the teacher's request to read from the textbook in the manner expected in a particular reading group—whether as a form of resistance or for other reasons—can have the consequence of assigning the student the identity of unruly, uneducable, learning disabled, naughty, or rebellious and can potentially lead to being expelled from the group or even the classroom and implicitly labeled as not-one-of-the-group, not-one-of-us, but one-of-"them." It is the discourse of reading pedagogy and schooling that makes such identity dynamics both possible and seemingly reasonable and ethical.

Discourse as Truth, Rationality, and Common Sense

By discourse as truth, rationality, and common sense we mean discourse as a system of concepts, ideas, and social practices, an ideology, that appears natural, obvious, and without question. As we mentioned in Chapter 1, when a discourse appears to be natural and common sense it exerts a kind of power that controls how people act, think, evaluate, interpret, feel, believe, and respond.

When a discourse is hegemonic, when it stands by itself as truth, common sense, and rationality, it promotes definitions of knowledge and argumentation in ways that hide, denigrate, or exclude other definitions of knowledge and argumentation. For example, consider the debate over what constitutes research on reading and what knowledge about reading is valid. The U.S. government established the National Reading Panel to decide what research showed about reading achievement in order to in-form educational policy at many levels. This would seem to be common sense. The National Reading Panel made a decision to include only studies that had characteristics they associated with high quality and that allowed the studies to be aggregated. This appears to be common sense. Similarly, the U.S. Department of Education took a stance that only certain types of research provided reliable and usable knowledge about reading education—the so-called scientific clinical studies. Again, the decision appears to be common sense. Yet, each instance of "common sense" privileged a limited set of definitions of reading and achievement, research studies, researchers, and ways of knowing and understanding, which framed reading instruction, reading assessment, and the allocation of funds for reading research and for reading instruction programs. What makes government policy around reading education and reading research so powerful is not just the allocation of resources around a particular approach to reading instruction, but rather the government's advocacy of a model of "common sense" and its marginalization of other ways of knowing, researching, and defining; its promulgation of a hegemonic discourse about reading and reading research. Those who take up ways of knowing, researching, and defining outside of what has been defined as "common sense" are at risk of being defined as lacking common sense and of being irrational. Children who fail to learn and achieve in the approved "scientifically based" reading instruction programs are provided identities that marginalize and stigmatize them—they may be labeled as learning disabled or as resistant to intervention. It is in creating the dividing line between the rational and common sense on one side and the irrational on the other that discourses exercise immense power. The investment of the state in particular discourses provides a way for the state to control what occurs within the state and to do so as a matter of common sense and rationality rather than as a matter of political initiative or of privileging a particular cultural politics or set of people. It provides a way for the state itself to become rationality itself, and disloyalty to the state and its policies becomes irrationality.

For researchers interested in discourse analysis, part of the analytic task is to examine how, what, and when a discourse becomes taken as truth, common sense and rationality, how it naturalizes that common sense, and rationality, how it marginalizes and obfuscates alternatives, and who is privileged by the truth, common sense, and rationality promoted by the discourse. It can be difficult to engage in such analysis, to acknowledge that we are all "captured" by dominant discourses to some extent. Researchers have to learn to see again (to "re-search") beyond what they have come to understand in their own lives as natural, common sense, and rational.

There are entry points for re-searching a dominant discourse and its rationality. First, since no discourse—no matter how dominant—is ever fully totalizing, there are always some contradictions and anomalies that are not adequately explained by the dominant discourse. Second, because dominant discourses privilege some at the expense of others, there is often resistance to such discourses. In order to guard themselves against "irrationality" and challenges to its common sense, an institution or the state itself must continuously engage in surveillance. One can examine where and how surveillance is maintained over people's actions as institutions. Researchers can examine the linguistic devices that discourses use to promote their rationality (see Lakoff & Johnson, 1980). For example, the metaphor of medicine and illness is often used in framing reading education: Students' strengths and weaknesses as readers are *diagnosed* so that they can receive the appropriate *treatment* or *intervention*. So naturalized is the metaphor of illness in reading pedagogy and research, that the use of medical technology for use in reading research seems natural and obvious.

Researchers can also examine how verbs are used within a discourse to suggest relationships among people as well as what is assumed to be universal truth. For example, analysis of transitivity can provide insights into assumptions about when people act on the world and when things just are. For example, consider the phrase, "Bob reads." Such a phrase might be uttered by a teacher to a parent or to another teacher in describing Bob's achievement level or a characteristic about Bob. But a closer look at that phrase might question whether or not "read" can actually be an intransitive verb—doesn't Bob have to read something? If *reads* is allowed to be an intransitive verb, then it becomes an attribute of a person rather than an activity. Questions can be asked about the implications of framing *reads* as an attribute of a person. Who is privileged by such framing, in what ways, and who is not?

Other devices can also be examined: nominalizations, active and passive constructions, the use of the present tense of the verb *to be*, the use of modals, and so on. Each of these linguistic devices provides an entry point for "re-searching" discourse, for making visible what is often hidden by assumptions of common sense and rationality.

Discourse as Literacy Curriculum

Whether stated or unstated, acknowledged or not, the use of discourse as a noun in the study of literacy events in classrooms implies a literacy curriculum. By *literacy curriculum* we mean curriculum in its broadest sense: formal and informal; explicit and hidden; academic, social, cultural, and political; planned and manifest; process and product. That is, what is taught and what is learned is a discourse or perhaps more accurately, a series of discourses and discourse orders (ordered relationships among discourse; cf. Fairclough, 1992) that constitute a discourse of literacy. We also include in our definition of curriculum a movement through time and space; by that we are referring to the planned movement of students and teacher through the designated curriculum as well as their actual movement through the manifest curriculum. That is, a curriculum involves a series of events and activities through which students and teachers must move, and that movement involves various conceptions of the relationship of time, space, and people; what Bakhtin (1935/1981) called chronotopes (for more discussion of classroom chronotopes see Bloome & Katz, 1997; Leander, 2004; Mahiri, 2004). In sum, a literacy curriculum is a discourse that students and teachers experience and acquire: a set of events, activities, texts, uses, identities, truths, and rationalities with which and through which students and teacher move. One purpose, then, of a discourse analysis of language and literacy events in classrooms is to describe the literacy curriculum as a discourse and what it does, to whom, when, where, and how.

Schematically, the organization of the four definitions of discourse as a noun listed earlier—discourse as text, as language-in-use, as identity, and as truth and rationality—is shown in Figure 2.1, which provides a heuristic for differentiating discourse analy-

Figure 2.1. Discourse as a noun and the study of literacy events in classrooms.

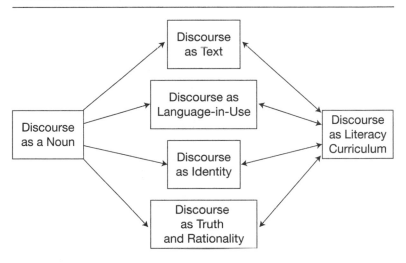

sis studies of language and literacy events in classrooms as well as a way to create a broader picture from a series of discourse analysis studies.

Within the context of literacy events in classrooms, we have argued that there are at least four concepts associated with discourse as a noun: discourse as text, discourse as language-in-use, discourse as identity, and discourse as truth, rationality, and common sense. We have suggested that each of these concepts can be examined heuristically at both a micro level and a macro level and that working across micro and macro levels provides theoretical insights not otherwise available. Also, we have framed the discussion of discourse as a noun to encourage discourse analysis as a process of "re-searching." Finally, we have argued that discourse analysis based on defining discourse as a noun implies an analysis of literacy curriculum where curriculum is not limited to acquisition of bits of knowledge and skills but with ways of knowing, definitions of knowledge, rationality, social identity, social hierarchy, power relations, ways of using spoken and written language, and ways of being.

Discourse as a Verb

Although rare, discourse can also be used as a verb, as in the following examples:

- They were discoursing the classroom into being.
- She was discoursing him as a hero.
- Stephen discoursed with Fred.

When used as a verb, discourse becomes a kind of action that a person or a group of people take with others. In the first example, discourse refers to the use of language to create an institutional space labeled *classroom.* In the second example, she was using language to define him as a hero; that is, she was using a linguistic and/or semiotic system to position him as a hero, presumably in relation to others. In these first two examples, discourse is a transitive verb, an action taken upon someone or something. But the last example illustrates a use of discourse as an intransitive verb. Stephen and Fred were in the state of being labeled "discoursing." We assume that they were "discoursing" something or someone (implied through ellipsis) and thereby argue that, as a verb, discourse is always a transitive verb. We take that position; discourse is always a transitive verb.

There is a sense in which our description of discourse as a verb is similar to uses of the phrase "discursive construction" (McHoul, 2001). Such similarities are stronger when discursive construction is itself a verb, as in "They were discursively constructing the classroom." What is at issue is not whether the characterization of discourse as a verb is fully distinct from other uses of discourse, but rather what questions we are able to or are more likely to ask by considering the various grammatical uses of discourse. By defining discourse as a verb we emphasize the concerted actions people take through language and related semiotic systems to create, maintain, challenge, circumvent, interpellate, resist, and transform the manifest ideologies and social, cultural, and economic tools of a social institution, including the relationships of people to each other and the movement of people through time and space. In other words, instead of viewing discourse as a set of concepts, structures, and practices, at either a micro level or macro level, *as a verb discourse can be viewed as actions that people and institutions take in response to each other; and more specifically, actions done with language and other semiotic systems* in order to create, recreate, change, and maintain identities, roles, and social contexts that people live within (and without). For the purposes of this chapter, we will concentrate on the role that literacy events in and related to schools and classrooms play in this action.

One advantage of defining discourse as a verb is the emphasis on the dynamic relationship of people and institutions to each other. The simple notion that people engage in discourse (that is to say, communicate with one another) is in fact complex when it is carefully examined, since at one level the teacher and students, even when they are sitting still, are moving through time and space while socially constructing how they as individuals and as a group will move through the time and space of the classroom as well as the time and space of the school as a social institution. As people engage in discoursing, they are acting in concert with their own lived histories with previous discourses. At the same time, they are socially constructing or reconstructing new discourses, figured worlds (cf. Holland, Cain, & Skinner, 1998), and negotiating how they as individuals or as a group will be moving in the future through the time and space of other social institutions such as family, community, and work.

Consider the classroom discussion of Alice Walker's short story "Everyday Use," described in the introduction and in Chapter 1. The reading and discussion of the short story took approximately 15 minutes. Each student stayed at his or her assigned desk, and the teacher primarily stayed seated on a stool at the front of the classroom—they occupied that space first by silently reading the story and then by engaging in a discussion of it with the postural configurations, body movements, verbal behaviors, and so on, deemed appropriate to such activities in their classroom. It is unlikely that when hanging out with friends outside of school, they act in the same manner. Through how they act and react to each other, they discourse that event, that social genre (a recitation classroom reading lesson), and the social institution in which the event and social genre are embedded (school) into being. In discoursing that event into being, the actions they take are built on a collective history of discoursing events in school settings.

Discoursing always involves a relationship with an activity that moves across time. On a particular Tuesday the teacher and students began a social event at 9:00 a.m., the beginning of the class period, and they ended the event at 9:57 a.m. (the end of the class period). Between 9:00 and 9:57 they discoursed. Yet there is a sense in which the use of the past tense is misleading. It is as if the teacher and students were able to come to completion. If we take the view that discoursing is a never completed action then the use of the past progressive tense is more appropriate than the use of the past tense. It is an action that is never fully completed, always subject to refraction either as a continuation or as taken up in future events. What an event means is always open to being renegotiated later.

Discoursing is a material, public activity in which people act on each other and the social institutions in which they live. It is not a state of being analogous to "They were meditating" or "They were existing." When framed as a verb, discoursing is an action even when it may not appear to be all that active. In the lesson on "Everyday Use," many of the students did not seem to participate. Yet, even the students in the class who remained silent were participating in discoursing the event, the lesson, and the classroom into being.

The phrase "discoursing on something" does not mean the same as "discussing such-and-such topic." Rather, to discourse *on* something means to act on that something, even if that something is only time and space. Thus the sentence, "The teacher and students were discoursing the lesson," is not the same as "The teacher and students were discussing the topic of the lesson." The latter refers to the limited action of the teacher and students exchanging comments about a particular topic. The former sentence refers to the teacher and students creating a public event labeled *lesson*. *Lesson* is a way to move through time and space, and within that movement the teacher and the students might be creating, maintaining, challenging, circumventing, interpellating, resisting, and transforming literary knowledge, their relationship to the school as a social institution, and their social relationships to each other.

Can it be the case that teachers and students can be engaged in discussing without also being engaged in discoursing? No. Whenever teachers and students are engaged in discussion, in exchanging comments and views on a topic, they are also engaged in acting on something, even if that something is only the filling up of time and space. The difference between discussing and discoursing is not in the actions of the participants but in the level of analysis implied by those describing the event.

Discoursing Things Into Being

As we have argued above, people use language (spoken, written, nonverbal actions, and other semiotic systems) to act and react to one another in order to discourse various figured worlds into being (Holland et al., 1998) and to adapt the situations in which they find themselves (Bandquedano-Lopez, Solis, & Kattan, 2005). With that theoretical premise in mind, the question we want to raise here is, Can literacy be constructed through the discoursing of people, or is the nature of the object that can be taken by *to discourse* limited to particular semantic categories that does not include "literacy"? More simply stated, does the use of discourse as a verb imply particular definitions of literacy?

As we have argued earlier in this chapter and in Chapter 1, through discoursing people construct social events, social identities, social structures, social statuses, histories, social practices, social spaces, and ways of moving through time and space. Each of these listed objects of discursive construction could involve written language (and related semiotic systems) in nontrivial ways and thus could be characterizable as "literate" or "literacy," as in literacy event, literate identity, literacy practice, and so on. Implied in each of these objects is that the object involves social relationships among people. These relationships may be face-to-face, at a geographical distance, over time (e.g., historical), between a person and a group, or among groups. Even the discoursing of a social identity assigned to an individual, such as member of the top reading group in the classroom or classroom trouble maker, is a social relationship. There cannot be a top reading group without having a bottom reading group. The student who has the social identity as a member of the top reading group has a particular kind of relationship with the members of that reading group and another set of relationships with members of other reading groups. The student labeled a trouble maker can only have such a social identity because of a social relationship with other students and the teacher.

Who Discourses?

In considering what affordances the use of discourse as a verb can provide to the study of literacy, it is helpful to examine a sentence such as the following:

The school was discoursing a cultural ideology for the neighborhood community.

The subject of the sentence above is "the school." It could refer to a specific school or it could be a broad gloss of schools in general as a social institution. For us, either definition of "the school" raises similar issues with regard to the verb to discourse. If "the school" refers to a specific school, we might assume that it is the teachers, students, staff, and other people involved in the school who are doing the discoursing, with "the school" being a shorthand way of indicating those people. But consider the definition of "the school" as a broad social institution. In many scholarly discussions, social institutions are frequently represented as being actors themselves, as if "the school" acts independently of the particular people who constitute the school as a social institution.

There are legitimate reasons for treating a social institution as if it acted on its own, independently of the people who constitute it. First, in dealing with a social institution like a school, it is often hard to figure out who is actually responsible for the actions of the school. For example, consider the ninth-grade language arts classroom and their discussion of "Everyday Use." The teacher in that classroom was required to give differentiated grades (A, B, C, D, F) to the students based on their academic performance over the previous 6 weeks. Students who did not complete their academic work and who did not pass their tests were failed and would have to repeat the English class. If one challenged the grading practice, the teacher would note that it was not her decision to grade students in such a manner, but she was following school policy; the principal would say that it is district policy; the administrators would refer one to the board of education whose members would refer both to the recommendations from the advisory committee of teachers, administrators, and parents who based their recommendations on advice from educational experts and practices at other school districts, and also to the needs and demands of university admission committees and employers who need the grading to differentiate student access. How does one refer to such an entangled network of bureaucracy of individuals and roles except by referencing the social institution, "the school"? A limitation of such a reference is that it contributes to the opaqueness of the social institution and the lack of responsibility that individuals associated with that social institution take for the social, cultural, political, and economic consequences of the actions taken through that social institution. Another limitation is that it tends to homogenize the social institution. For example, there are classrooms and schools where there are alternatives to traditional grading practices. In some cases these alternatives exist alongside traditional grading practices; in other cases the traditional grading practices have been supplanted. The issue here is not about grading practices, but about assigning the agency of discoursing to nonhuman entities. In brief, in sentences like "the school was discoursing a cultural ideology for the neighborhood community" when "the school" is a specific school and the phrase is a shorthand means of referring to the various people affiliated with the school, then human agency is maintained. But when "the school" refers to a broad social institution that is assumed to stand beyond the people who constitute it, human agency is made opaque and the lived spaces of people within and affected by that social institution are homogenized.

What Is Discoursed?

In this section we examine the relationship of the verb *to discourse* and its object in that same sentence:

The school was discoursing a cultural ideology for the neighborhood community.

The object of the verb, of course, is "cultural ideology" and its modifying phrase. Cultural ideologies about the neighborhood community do not just happen; they are realized as people act and react to their material world. Regardless of how an administrator, teacher, or individual staff member privately thinks about the neighborhood community, cultural ideologies are taken up, rejected, or accepted when they become visible and tangible. That

is, cultural ideologies (including the projection of a cultural ideology onto others) become visible in the material world through
objects such as the signs that are posted on the school walls, the
memos and newsletters that are sent home to parents, the spatial
location of the school in relation to the community, the conversations school personnel have with each other and people outside
of the school, the school curriculum, and the types of classes and
activities that are offered both for parents and students during
and after school.

It is through such material evidence that discourse shifts from
being a static, esoteric concept to being a verb and an action. For
example, sending a memo home to parents regarding a workshop
that is being offered on effective parenting practices is an action,
and it creates a cultural ideology about the neighborhood community that suggests the community is lacking parenting skills; it positions the neighborhood community as deficit and the school as
addressing that deficit. The school is providing a forum in which
the parents in the community can become more effective parents.
The issue here is that for a cultural ideology to be realized it must
move from inside the circle of the school administrators, teachers,
and counselors privately believing that the parents in the community need parenting classes to the act of creating a workshop on
effective parenting or otherwise making visible such characterization, either explicitly or implicitly. The message being sent to the
community is that there is a lack of knowledge that exists in this
particular community about how to be a good parent. In brief, the
school is discoursing a cultural ideology about and for the neighborhood community.

But who decides what and who is a good parent and what
are effective parenting practices? What does it mean to be a good
parent in a particular community? Would an effective parenting
workshop be offered to parents who live in an upper-middle-class
community? A way to explore the promulgation of cultural ideologies about and for a neighborhood community is to compare the
previous example with a school that does not explicitly discourse
a deficit cultural ideology about and for their neighborhood community. For example, consider a school in an upper-middle-class
community. For the purpose of this illustration, assume that the
school does not offer parenting skills classes or other similar workshops and services. Also assume that there is minimal explicit,

formal communication between the school and the neighborhood community. One might argue that this school is not discoursing any cultural ideology about or for the neighborhood community; after all, there appear to be few, if any, overt actions being taken by the school in discoursing with others about the neighborhood community. Yet we would argue that nonetheless the school is discoursing a cultural ideology about and for the neighborhood community since that school and its community exist within a broader context that includes itself and the school that offered parenting classes. It is the contrast, the absence of actions that discourses a cultural ideology for the neighborhood community, a cultural ideology that designates the parenting practices of the neighborhood community as healthy. This absence is as material and real as the actions of the other school in producing communications to the home, workshops, and newsletters.

The discussion above illustrates how schools can discourse a cultural ideology about and for the neighborhood community through the actions or non-actions they take when acting and re-acting to the neighborhood community. The point we are making here is that schools (and the people associated with them) are not passive agents. They actively create, re-create, contest, and support cultural ideologies about the neighborhood community.

Who Is Discoursed?

Consider a sentence such as:

The teacher and students were discoursing various social identities for themselves.

Psychological descriptions sometimes characterize a person's identity as a set of personal traits that change little over time or in varying social contexts. However, rather than viewing identity as fixed, here we are assuming that identity is interactionally and socially constructed as particular situations are constructed: In other words, the constitution of the person is part of the social construction of the event. Thus social identity is far from stable. Instead, people's identities are continually being constructed and reconstructed as they interact with one another. This view of social identity is similar to Gergen's (1999) notion of "self as relationship." Gergen acknowledges the difficulty in talking about identity as socially constructed when most people are accustomed to thinking of identity as individual: "We must locate a way of understanding ourselves as constituents of a process that eclipses any individual within it, but is simultaneously constituted by its individual elements" (p. 129). If social identities are constructed through people's relationships with one another, and if discourse as a verb is defined as actions people take in response to one another, then part of what people do is discourse social identities.

Teachers and students continually engage in discoursing social identities in classrooms. The transcript below is part of a class discussion in which students in a college-level basic writing class were discussing an incident that had occurred at a local hospital. A patient's husband had insisted on choosing the medical staff who would be assisting during his wife's operation. The incident had been reported in the local media and had received widespread attention because the patient's husband had dictated that all surgical staff must be white. During the class discussion, several students argued that the husband, because he was paying for the surgery, had the right to choose the surgical staff—based on any criteria that he chose. George, an adult student who worked in the field of health care, disagreed.

301 *George:* you come to the hospital
302 I don't care what your husband think
303 My job
304 is to make sure that you come out of that operation
305 in the, in the,
306 as best
307 you possibly can out of the operation.
308 Now,
309 *Teacher:* In other words, it's your ability to do the job.
310 *George:* That's right.
311 And if this lady here (*pointing to a fellow student*)
312 this is my assistant,
313 I know she's the best I got on staff,
314 I don't care if she's blue.
315 If she the best I got,
316 that's the best shot I got to make sure you okay,
317 I'm sorry about the husband
318 cause my job is to make sure you come out of that,

319　come out of there alive.
320　*Mark:* And who paying you though?
321　But you got to (*indecipherable*)
322　*George:* As a surgeon,
323　you can't think about that.

In this segment of the class discussion, George positions his audience—his teacher and classmates—as hypothetical patients and himself as a doctor. George uses and stresses first person ("My job") in line 303 to position himself as an expert in the world of health care and second person ("you come to the hospital") in line 301 to position his listeners as patients. In lines 304–307, George continues to position his audience as hypothetical patients and himself as a health care provider. He even positions a fellow student ("this lady here") as his assistant in lines 311–312. Mark, in lines 320–321, uses second person to affirm George's social position as surgeon: "And who paying you though?" In lines 322–323, George speaks for all surgeons when he says, "As a surgeon, you can't think about that."

This one classroom event was not an isolated example. The class had engaged in discoursing the social identity of health care expert for George on numerous occasions during the semester: "We'll have to ask George about that" became a common refrain. Because George struggled with the mechanics of academic writing, this discoursing of a positive social identity allowed him to serve, at least some of the time, as a knowledgeable expert. Walkerdine (1990) has argued that people are "not unitary subjects uniquely positioned, but are produced as a nexus of subjectivities, in relations of power which are constantly shifting, rendering them at one moment powerful and at another powerless" (p. 3).

Basic writing students, like George, are often characterized as "other" and are sometimes portrayed as deviant, resistant, and even childlike. Such characterizations can serve to maintain power inequities in educational institutions. If we only knew George through his writing, we would probably not be able to see the dynamic agent who was often able to position himself as an expert in class discussions. As Gray-Rosendale (2000) has noted, basic writing students are active agents who often position themselves in ways that run counter to scholarly constructions of basic writers as academically marginalized, victimized, and educationally lacking.

Discoursing as Narrating a Literacy Identity

Sfard and Prusak (2005) argue for an operational definition of identity that *"equate[s] identities with stories about person"* (p. 14, emphasis in original). They write:

> ... we suggest that identities may be defined as collections of stories about persons or, more specifically, as those narratives about individuals that are reifying, endorsable, and significant. The reifying quality comes with the use of verbs such as be, have or can rather than do, and with the adverbs always, never, usually, and so forth, that stress repetitiveness of actions. A story about a person counts as endorsable if the identity-builder, when asked would say that it faithfully reflects the state of affairs in the world. A narrative is regard as significant if any change in it is likely to affect the storyteller's feelings about the identified person. The most significant stories are often those that imply one's membership in, or exclusions from, various communities. (pp. 16–17)

What is of interest to Sfard and Prusak is not the enumeration and description of identities, but rather the process of identity-building, what they label "identifying" (p. 16) and the "complex dialectic between identity-building and other human activities" (p. 17).

Given Sfard and Prusak's operational definition of identity, a sentence can be viewed as a process of identifying, of constructing a set of narratives. Consider the following sentence:

They are discoursing a literate social identity for Susan

At least one of these narratives is about Susan. But there is another narrative being constructed, a narrative about being literate. That is, "They" are constructing a narrative that reifies and stabilizes actions that count as being literate; these actions that count as being literate may be a single occurring action (e.g., "Susan passed the reading test; she is now literate.") or they may be repetitive actions (e.g., "Susan is a literate person; she reads the newspaper every morning"). Following Sfard and Prusak's discussions of identity as narrative, these actions that count as being literate are endorsable by the identity-builders; the equation of the actions and the narratives in which they are embedded represent the identity-builders' view of the world. In sum, any assignment of a literate identity always requires both the production of at least two narratives, one for the person/people and one about what counts as being literate, and also that these narratives are endorsable and significant for those producing the narratives.

We can assume that there are multiple and differing narratives for what counts as being literate. Some of these narratives may be complementary and others may conflict. Indeed, we would argue that much of what passes for scholarship in literacy studies concerns which of these narratives of being literate are legitimate (in Sfard and Prusak's terms, which ones are candidates to be "endorsable") and which narratives supersede or incorporate other narratives (e.g., a narrative about literate identities and passing a literacy test can be incorporated into a narrative about literacy skills being a set of cognitive skills that all members of society need to be productive citizens and have a good life). But the debate over which narratives are endorsable and which significant overlooks the question of how it is that any narrative becomes endorsable. In part, it is a question about who has the rights and privileges to endorse a narrative and who does not, and in part, it is a question of how those rights and privileges have been allocated. We can label this dynamic *entitlement* (cf. Shuman, 1997): in brief, who is entitled to tell what stories, when, where, with whom, and to whom; and who is entitled to endorse and designate as significant which narratives, told by whom, when, where, with whom, and to whom.

It is the question of entitlement that is especially important to questions of discoursing because entitlement is often implied and can be delegated. For example, consider a first-grade classroom that is using one of the reading programs designated by the government as scientifically based. Let's assume that one or more of the students do not engage in the behaviors designated by the reading program as constituting adequate progress toward being literate but that many of the children do. Who is entitled to tell what narratives about what is occurring in this classroom, to whom, when, where, and how? Who is entitled to endorse such narratives and how do such narratives gain significance? Although we can imagine that there are multiple narratives that can and that might be told, we can also imagine that some of those narratives carry more significance than others. In all likelihood, the teacher is entitled to tell a narrative about a few students who lacked the ability to acquire the skills provided through the reading program. She obtains this entitlement from the people in the government through their designation of the reading program as scientifically based and from the bureaucracy and organizational structure of the school which has supported her use of the reading program and monitored her implementation of the reading program. Indeed, we can view the teacher as having been delegated by the government the entitlement to tell that narrative. But suppose the narrative the teacher tells is that the reading program is awful, does not work, that the students who did well would have done well regardless of the reading program, and that the students would have all been better off if they had spent the year in the school library reading from the children's literature collection there. Of this narrative we can ask, who has endorsed it other than the teacher? If the teacher is alone in endorsing the narrative, then the teacher may not have an entitlement to tell the narrative. Indeed, at least in some schools and in some school districts, teachers are only entitled to tell those narratives that have been endorsed by their superiors within the school system; and to the degree that the school system is aligned with the local, state, or federal governments' manifest ideologies regarding literacy education (as expressed through policies and funding), those superiors in the school system are delegates for the government. The point we want to make here is that "discoursing a literate social identity" is an action that takes place in relationship to state ideologies about being literate and that relationship might be one of delegation or of resistance.

Hidden in the discussion above is an unstated assumption that narratives about "being literate" are uncontestable. That is, although there may be differing and conflicting narratives about being literate, the idea of being literate is nearly universally endorsed. Yet, a number of literacy researchers have questioned that idea. If literacy is defined as an event in which the use of written language (or related semiotic systems) is more than trivial, then being literate as an individual's identity is a non sequitur: People are not literate or illiterate; they are participants in literacy events. Which literacy events people participate in may vary, and how they participate in various literacy events may vary, but they themselves are not literate or illiterate.

One way to frame the issue is that a group of researchers have questioned whether one set of narratives of being literate should be endorsed. That is, it cannot be denied that there exist narratives that identify people as being literate or not literate and that these narratives have various endorsements and entitlements. So, what is at question is the basis upon which endorsements of such narratives are entitled. Thus, analysis of narratives identifying being literate involve not just the being literate narrative itself but the narratives that support their endorsements and entitlements.

It matters little, we believe, whether researchers ever use discourse as a verb in their writings. What does matter is how they and others conceptualize the process of discoursing. Although Reisigl & Wodak (2001) do not use *discourse* as a verb in their own writing, they define *discourse* in a way similar to how we are suggesting it might be defined as a verb:

> I understand discourse as institutionalized language behavior, this language behavior determines actions and possesses power. This discourse is also real, constitutes reality. . . . Consequently, discourse does not manifest actions: *it is action.* (p. 27, emphasis added)

If discourse is conceptualized as an action, then the researcher can foreground questions such as the following when analyzing classroom language and literacy events:

1. What kind of action(s) is(are) the discoursing of language and literacy events within a particular classroom event or set of classroom events?
2. How does the discoursing define and constitute a language and literacy event in the classroom?
3. What is being discoursed within a language and literacy event?
4. Who is discoursing?
5. What and who is being acted upon through the discoursing?
6. What narratives of identity are being constructed through the discoursing and what consequences do these narratives have?

Variations in the Discourse Analysis of a Classroom Language and Literacy Event

In this chapter we present four different approaches to the discourse analysis of a language and literacy event in a ninth-grade language arts classroom, the discussion of "Everyday Use" that opens this book. Mandy Smith provides a discourse analysis from an interactional sociolinguistic perspective, Susan Goldman from a sociocognitive perspective, Douglas Macbeth from an ethnomethodological perspective, and Stephanie Carter from a black feminist research perspective.

Presenting (and reading) four discourse analyses of the same target event is not a simple matter. At one level, the four analyses give four different perspectives of what appears to be the same event. But at another level, it is not really the same event that they are analyzing. They contextualize the target lesson segment differently, and they focus on different aspects of the target segment (highlighting the fact that classroom events are not monolithic experiences).

We begin with a brief description of the event that we asked the four researchers to analyze.

BACKGROUND TO THE EVENT

The event was taken from one lesson of a ninth-grade language arts classroom early in the academic year. The classroom was located in a Grades 8 through 12 magnet school focusing on literature located in a large urban school district in the southern United States. Admission to the magnet school was not based on academic performance but on a lottery of those who expressed interest in attending the school. The students in the classroom varied widely in academic performance. There were 22 students in the class: 9 male, 13 female, 14 white, 8 African American. Figure 3.1provides a map of the classroom. The teacher was Latina, her family originally from South America. She was in her third year of teaching. She was highly regarded by the principal and her colleagues and already had a good reputation among the students in the school.

The curriculum during the early part of the year focused on the novel *The House on Mango Street* by Sandra Cisneros (1984). The students would read a chapter in that novel and then read other literary works related to the topic of the chapter. The teacher also had the students engage in various written assignments from creative works to analytic essays to formal grammar assignments. In the particular unit from which the event was taken, the students had read the chapter from *The House on Mango Street* on the

Figure 3.1. Floor plan of classroom.

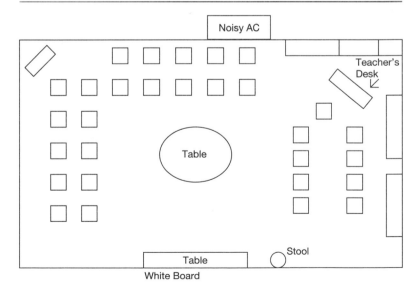

protagonist's name and had been discussing for several days the impact and nature of people's names. The previous day they had read a chapter from Billie Letts's novel *Where the Heart Is* (2004) and had been assigned the homework task of writing an imaginary conversation between the protagonists of the two books regarding the nature and use of names. Earlier in the target lesson some of the students had read aloud and performed their creative conversations, which had led to a general discussion about the impact of names. The teacher had passed out a copy of Alice Walker's short story "Everyday Use," which is about an African American woman, Dee (who had changed her name to Wangero), who has returned home to visit her mother and sister after receiving an education and becoming more aware of her black heritage. The teacher had the students silently read the story with the instruction to look for the purposes of a name change. They had begun the discussion.

The event we asked Smith, Goldman, Macbeth, and Carter to analyze from their different discourse analysis perspectives came after the teacher had focused discussion on the question "Why do people change their names?" and the discussion segued to the question "What kind of a person is Dee?" The event occurs 55 minutes into the 60-minute lesson. We provided each scholar a video recording of the event as well as the transcript presented below and offered to provide any additional information we had available that they might request. Since any transcript already imposes a theoretical perspective on an event, we encouraged the scholars to modify the transcript to facilitate their analysis, and we encouraged them to focus on the whole or any part of the event best suited to how they would approach a discourse analysis.

The task we asked of the four scholars was not an easy one. If they had undertaken the original study, they might have selected a different event and different classroom to analyze, one that would have allowed them to investigate issues of current concern to their field and program of research. They might have selected an event from a setting with which they were more familiar. They might have pointed the video camera and audio recorder in different directions. And, they might have selected a broader unit of analysis or incorporated knowledge of other aspects of the classroom, school, and community into their analysis, perhaps interviewing the teacher and students in order to gain further insight

Figure 3.2. Transcription symbols.

↑ = rising intonation at end of utterance	⌐ line 1
	= overlap
↓ = falling intonation	∟ line 2
XXXX = undecipherable	vowel+ = elongated vowel
<u>stress</u>	* = voice, pitch, or style change
"reading from written text"	*words* = boundaries of a voice, pitch, or style change
▼ = less volume	
▲ = more volume	*Nonverbal behavior or transcriber comments for clarification purpose in italics*
▲▲ = greatly increased volume	
<u>uttered with increased speed</u>	Line number is prefaced with the minute of the lesson the transcript begins.
| = short pause ||| = long pause	
𝕀 = interrupted by the next line	
- = uncompleted word	

and triangulation.[1] As important, the rhetorical framing of their analyses differs. That is, there is variation in how they construct the relationship between data analysis and theory building and how they conceptualize their audience. Finally, these four scholars are not representing their fields per se, but rather representing their own approach to discourse analysis as a participant in different disciplinary fields.

The transcript of the event begins at 55 minutes and 25 seconds into the lesson (refer to Figure 3.2 for a list of the symbols and notations used here):

55-01 *Teacher:* very good ↓ *points at Arnold*
55-02 so what kind of a person is Dee ↑ *T makes a downward movement with both hands as she says "Dee"*
55-03 \| \| *(2.5 seconds)*
55-04 ▼ Valerie *T points with left hand to Valerie*
55-05 *Valerie:* she wants to be something she's not ↓ *volume decreases to nearly inaudible*
55-06 *Teacher:* ▲ <u>ok</u> she wants to be something she's <u>no+t</u> \|

55-07 ummmmm

55-08 because she wants nice things ↑or ↓

55-09 or |

55-10 wha- why why do you say that ↑

55-11 *Unidentified student:* ⌈xxxxxxxxxxxxxxxxxxxxxxxx

55-12 *Valerie:*   ⌊just the way she acts she
       doesn't want | to | increased volume from V's
       previous utterance, increased speed

55-13 anybody know she likes to have |

55-14 all | house | and |

55-15 she likes to buy things that they can't afford ↓

55-16 *Teacher:* ok

55-17 *buy things they can't afford*

55-18 Rita you had a comment

55-19 *Rita:* xxxx

55-20 *Teacher:*   and then we'll get

55-21 *Rita:* I think she's kind of sel+fish+

55-22 *Teacher:* ok

55-23 why ↑

55-24 *Unidentified student:* xxxxxxxxxxxxxxx

55-25 *Rita:* ▼ I just feel that xxxxxx ↓ *volume decreases to
       inaudible*

55-26 *Teacher:* ▲ you'll learn is why is my favorite
                          ⌈question

55-27 *Rita:* ▲   ⌊because she wants more than she has

55-28 ▼ so she's always asking her to get more

55-29 ▼ and xxxxxxx not and she's always over there just

55-30 embarrassed when she shouldn't be *you know* ↓

55-31 *Teacher:* ▲▲ so it's a <u>bad</u> thing to go for what you
       want ↑

55-32 *Valerie:* No

55-33 *Unidentified student:* No

55-34 *Rita:* no+↑

55-35 *Teacher:* I'm playin devil's   ⌉ advocate here

55-36 *Rita:*   ⌊ xxxx be embarrassed if
       | *slows speed* ▼ your family is like that and you're not
       * you know *↓

55-37 ▼you should at least share or something ↓

55-38 *Teacher:* ok ok

55-39 <u>Eve</u> what's your comment here
55-40 *Eve:* uhh
55-41 I think that it's goo+d to go | for more |
55-42 but <u>at</u> the same ti+me
55-43 don't make your family be ashamed of you+ |
55-44 ▼ like ummm
55-45 I think she wants to change herself because |
55-46 she | |
55-47 she's not satisfied with |
55-48 the way she | was brought up ↑ |
55-49 the way she had
55-50 when she was in France xxxxxxx *whatever*
55-51 and |
55-52 ▼ I just think that she was not satisfied |
55-53 she wants | |
55-54 to be something different |
55-55 something that excites her
55-56 *yeah * ↓
55-57 *Teacher:* <u>something</u> that excites her |
55-58 that's a very good comment |
55-59 I like that ↓ |
55-60 good
55-61 we'll go Ron *has his hand up*
55-62 we'll get back to that soon ↓
55-63 *Ron:* I kinda |
55-64 kinda think she wants to be kinda like |
55-65 pretending like this her life is kinda like a tree |
55-66 she wants to be at the <u>top</u> of the tree but yet |
55-67 she also tries to forget the <u>roots of it</u> at the same time
55-68 so she has to <u>keep</u> |
55-69 like the roots are what made her what she is right now |
55-70 and if she if she didn't have the roots to support her
       she wouldn't have anything to actually go for
55-71 so she has |
55-72 wants to be better than her family |
55-73 but yet she can't forget about her family either ↓
55-74 *Teacher:* <u>no</u> |
55-75 she can't |
55-76 good job ↓ |

55-77   ┌and
55-78 *Many students:*   └xxxxxx ┐ xxxx
55-79 *Teacher:*   └ ▲ we'll get
55-80 ▲ we'll get back
55-81 It's very philosophical
55-82 where life is like a tree
55-83 you made a metaphor
55-84 for xxxx
55-85 for life is a tree
55-86 or you could make a <u>simile</u> |
55-87 you said life is like a tree right ↑
55-88 ok we'll get we'll get more into similes
55-89 what I have is on the board for a couple of days
55-90 but the class discussion has been so interesting that I
         haven't been able to get to it
55-91 <u>Rachel</u>
55-92 *Rachel:* I think it's like
55-93 there is nothing wrong with going after your go+als
55-94 but going after fantasies is a whole different thing
55-95 when you have your goals you know where you are
         going from and where getting to
55-96 <u>but</u> fantasies you are always thinking about
         something
55-97 where you want to be
55-98 xxxxxxxxxxxxxxxxxxxxxxxx *classroom noise near the
         microphone made her utterance inaudible*
55-99 reminds me
55-100 you know that short story the necklace ↑
55-101 *Teacher:* <u>yes</u>
55-102 *Rachel:* that reminds me of the xxxxxxxxxxxxxxxxxxx
         *classroom noise near the microphone made her utterance
         inaudible*
55-103 *Teacher:* very good |
55-104 very good lots of different |
55-105 lots of different |
55-106 ummmmm |
55-107 <u>texts</u> |
55-108 becoming into
55-109 we have Breakfast at Tiffany's and xxxxxxxxxx
55-110 the necklace and all of that

55-111 uh tomorrow
55-112 bring your <u>conversations</u> *decreased speed*
55-113 you are going to turn those <u>in</u>
55-114 with another story ok ↑
55-115 so keep on to those ↓
55-116 keep on to those ↓
55-117 *Lori:* xxxxxxxx
55-118 *Teacher:* uh *to Lori*
55-119 you don't have the story <u>yet</u> *to Lori*
55-120 you don't have the story yet
55-121 we'll work on this tomorrow
55-122 alright ↑
55-123 uh
55-124 bring these tomorrow *T holds up a sheet of paper taken from the center table*
55-125 bring all the | the | of the stories that we have read so far
55-126 *S?:* notebooks right
55-127 *Teacher:* tomorrow
55-128 and your notebooks and pens and all that ↓
55-129 alright *have a great day*
55-130 *Students get up from desks and leave class*

The lesson ends at 59 minutes and 9 seconds.

An Interactional Sociolinguistic Perspective on an Instructional Conversation: Talking Opportunities for Literacy Learning into Being

Mandy Smith

My approach to a discourse analysis of the classroom segment builds on theories in sociolinguistic ethnography (cf. Gumperz, 1986; Hymes, 1974), interactional sociolinguistics applied to educational settings (cf. Bloome et al., 2005; Green & Wallat, 1981), and recent discussions of discourse analysis that bridge the micro- and macrocontexts of students lives in and out of classrooms (e.g., Bloome & Clark, 2006; Gee, 1996). Three theoretical principles guide this analysis:

1. Through how people act and react to each other, people construct what they are doing, what it means, who they are, and what the social significance of the event they are creating is; and the primary tool they use in constructing events, meanings, identities, and social significance is language.
2. Through their interactions, people construct relationships between and among texts, events, and contexts; these processes are known as the social construction of intertextuality and intercontextuality, respectively.
3. Part of what teachers and students create through their interactions are opportunities for learning.

One implication of these principles is that describing what happens in a classroom literacy event requires attention to the moment-by-moment unfolding of the event and how people build on each other's actions and uses of language (cf. Green & Wallat, 1981). At the same time, just as people must signal to each other how they interpret each other's actions and communicate their intentions, they must also signal to each other connections between the event they are constructing and future and previous events. The moment-by-moment unfolding and signaling of interpretations, intentions, and relationships to other events and contexts are the means by which people construct a shared, in situ definition of *learning* and create opportunities for that learning.

As people interact with each other, they construct a working consensus about what they are doing, a sort of enacted narrative, which they signal to each other through verbal, nonverbal, prosodic, and other communicative means (what Gumperz, 1986, has called "contextualization cues"). Since people must make these signals available and visible to each other, they are also available to researchers observing and participating in the event. What a researcher needs to do is document and then describe the signals (the contextualization cues) that the interlocutors themselves are using to construct a shared narrative, a shared sense about what they are collectively doing.

Green and Wallat (1981) provide a series of principles and tools for making such a description, and I have followed their work in my analysis here. In brief, I divided the video recording into a series of "message units" (similar to utterances), Interactional Units (a set of message units that are interactionally related and connected such as a question and answer or a teacher question followed by a student response followed by a teacher evaluation of the student response), and sets of related Interactional Units. Following Green and Wallat (1981), I based the boundaries of these units on the public behaviors of the interlocutors as they made clear to each other where the boundaries were (see example in Table 3.1). These bounded units—message units, Interactional Units, and sequences and series of Interactional Units—can be viewed metaphorically as the conversational building blocks that people in interaction with each other use in coconstructing what they are doing in classrooms and other educational settings and in co-constructing opportunities for learning.

Since my interest was on how the teacher and students together created learning opportunities, I focused attention on what counted as knowledge and how the teacher and students created opportunities to construct knowledge. In brief, this meant looking for how the teacher and students built on each other's message units in a way that defined what counted as knowledge in the lesson and on opportunities to extend the knowledge already presented. In some cases, this meant examining how the teacher and students defined what counted as reading and as evidence for an argument or claim.

Figure 3.3 provides a graphic representation of how these issues evolved during the lesson. The are three Interactional Units shown in this figure, set off by heavy black lines. I provide a detailed description of what happens within each Interactional Unit.

Interactional Unit 1 (Lines 55-02–55-17)

In line 55-02, the teacher asks the question of the class, "So what kind of a person is Dee?" She is opening this portion of the discussion by asking the class to make a claim about a character in the text. This is a new topic as the instructional task had been to identify reasons for changing one's name. The teacher is asking the students to make a claim about the ethical character of Dee and then warrant that claim with evidence from the text: Warranting claims with evidence from the text is the explicit goal of the lesson.

After 2.5 seconds of wait time, the teacher calls on a student, signaling her permission to speak by pointing with her left hand

Table 3.1. Message unit and interactional unit boundaries.

Line#	Speaker	Message Unit	Conextualization Cues that Mark Message Unit Boundaries	Contextualization Cues that Mark Interactional Unit Boundaries
55-01	Teacher	very good ↓ *points at Arnold*	End of message unit signaled by ceasing pointing at Arnold and drop in intonation pattern.	
55-02		so what kind of a person is Dee ↑ *T makes a downward movement with both hands as she says "Dee"*	Beginning of message unit marked by new intonation pattern, increase in delivery speed and use of verbal marker "so". End of message unit signaled by hand movement and rising intonation pattern associated with a question.	Initiates new topic through the use of a question
55-03		‖ *(2.5 seconds)*	Pause signals end of previous message unit and opportunity for students to bid for a turn at talk.	Maintains topic and interactional unit through silence waiting for someone to respond
55-04		▼ Valerie *T points with left hand to Valerie*	Drop in volume and pointing defines boundaries of the message unit.	Maintains topic and interactional unit by identifying a person to respond to question in 55-02
55-05	Valerie	she wants to be something she's not ↓ *volume decreases to nearly inaudible*	New speaker indicates new message unit; drop in volume indicates end of message unit.	Provides an answer to the question in 55-02 which maintains the topic and interactional unit
55-06	Teacher	▲ ok she wants to be something she's no+t ‖	New speaker indicates new message unit; verbal marker shows beginning of message unit (ok); elongation of vowel in last word (no+t) indicates end of message unit.	Signals acceptance of the answer by affirming it (ok) and repeating the answer. Ends interactional unit by accepting answer and signals the end through the use of the elongated vowel
55-07		ummmmm	Place holder	Holds right to the floor
55-08		because she wants nice things ↑ or ↓	Rise in volume followed by drop in volume indicates opening for a new speaker to have a turn at talk.	Initiates new topic with a new question

in lines 55-03 and 55-04. Valerie makes a claim about Dee in line 55-04, saying that "she wants to be something she's not." Valerie is giving a statement of opinion about the character. The teacher validates Valerie's claim by saying, "OK" and repeating her claim in line 55-06. Although the teacher validates the student's claim, she then asks for evidence to support this claim in lines 55-08 through 55-10 when she says, "because she wants nice things . . . or . . . wha- why why do you say that?" In response to the teacher's request for evidence about Valerie's claim that Dee wants to be something she is not, Valerie responds by saying, "just the way she acts (line 55-12) . . . she likes to buy things she can't afford" (line 55-15). It may look as though this is another claim about what kind of person Dee is because she is talking about what Dee likes, rather than making a claim that directly references the text they had been reading. However, in lines 55-16 and 55-17, the teacher responds to Valerie's comments by saying, "OK, buy things they can't afford." These are interpretable as validations of Valerie's comments. Because she repeats what Valerie has just said, it is reasonable within the context of the classroom to view the teacher as accepting Valerie's attempt to give evidence for her previous statement that Dee "wants to be something she's not." By accepting Valerie's evidence, the teacher is also accepting Valerie's initial claim about Dee. In line 55-18, the teacher ends this particular Interactional Unit by requesting that Rita share her comment.

Interactional Unit 1 can be viewed as an extended form of the traditional classroom conversational structure of teacher initiation followed by student response followed by teacher evaluation (hereafter IRE). The teacher asks a question in line 55-02, which is followed by a student response, which the teacher keeps open and scaffolds (lines 55-05 to 55-15), which is finally evaluated in line 55-16 and 55-17. There are two theoretical points to make about this conversational structure. First, it is adaptable. The teacher and students adapt it to their own uses. Some researchers have criticized the IRE conversational structure as limiting student contribution and requiring low-level, short-answer responses from students. While that may be so in some cases, the data in the transcript analyzed here shows that the teacher and students work within the IRE conversational structure in ways that allow for extended response and higher level thinking and argumentation. The adaptability of IRE conversational structures suggests that perhaps most

Figure 3.3. A representation of opportunities to learn in three interactional units

Line #	SP	Message Unit	What Counts as Knowledge			Defining Reading	Other
			Personal Preference Philosophy	Claim	Evidence		
55-02	T	so what kind of a person is Dee ↑ *T makes a downward movement with both hands as she says "Dee"*					
55-03		‖ *(2.5 seconds)*					
55-04		▼ Valerie *T points with left hand to Valerie*					
55-05	V	she wants to be something she's not ↓ *volume decreases to nearly inaudible*					
55-06	T	▲ <u>ok</u> she wants to be something she's <u>no+t</u> ‖					
55-07		Ummmmm					
55-08		because she wants nice things ↑ or ↓					
55-09		or ‖					
55-10		wha- why why do you say that ↑					
55-11		⌈ xxxxxxxxxxxxxxxx					
55-12	R	⌊ <u>just the way she acts she doesn't</u> want ‖ to ‖ *increased volume from V's previous utterance, increased speed*					
55-13		<u>anybody know she likes to have</u> ‖					
55-14		all ‖ house ‖ and ‖					
55-15		she likes to buy things that they can't afford ↓					
55-16	T	Ok					
55-17		*buy things they can't afford*					

Figure 3.3. *Continued*

55-18	T	Rita you had a comment						
55-19		XXXX						
55-20		and then we'll get						
55-21	RI	I think she's kind of selfish						
55-22	T	Ok						
55-23		Why						
55-24	RI	XXXXXXXXXX						
55-25		I just feel that XXXXX						
55-26	T	You'll learn why is my favorite question						
55-27	RI	Because she wants more than she has						
55-28		So she's always asking her to get more						
55-29		And XXXX not and she's always over there just						
55-30		Embarrassed when she shouldn't be you know						
55-31	T	So it's a bad thing to go for what you want						
55-32	RI	No						
55-33		No						
55-34		No						
55-35		I XXXX						
55-36		XXXX be embarrassed if your family is like that you you're not you know						
55-37		You should at least share or something						
55-38	T	Ok ok						
55-39	T	Eve what's your comment here						
55-40	E	Uhhh						

Figure 3.3. *Continued*

55-41		I think that its good to go for more	■					
55-42		But at the same time	■					
55-43		Don't make your family be ashamed of you	■					
55-44		Like ummm						
55-45		I think she wants to change herself because		■				
55-46		She						
55-47		She's not satisfied with		■				
55-48		They way she was brought up		■				
55-49		The way she had						
55-50		When she was in France XXXXXX *whatever*			■			
55-51		And						
55-52		I just think that she was not satisfied		■				
55-53		She wants						
55-54		To be something different		■				
55-55		Something that excites her		■				
55-56		yeah		■				
55-57	T	Something that excites her		⬭				
55-58		That's a very good comment		⬭				
55-59		I like that	⬭	⬭				
55-60		good		⬭				

Teacher Initiation	⬭	Boundary of Interactional Unit	▬▬▬	
Teacher Statement	⬭	Student Utterance	■	
Teacher Feedback/Evaluation	⬭			

if not all conversational structures also may be adaptable. If so, one implication for discourse analysis of language and literacy events in classrooms is the importance of asking how the teacher and students adapt extant conversational structures rather than asking what conversational structures are extant. The second theoretical point to make about IRE conversational structures based on Interactional Unit 1 is that what counts as knowledge is not necessarily fixed by an IRE conversational structure.

Interactional Unit 2 (Lines 55-18–55-38)

It is not only because a new student has the floor and has taken a turn at talk that a new Interactional Unit is signaled. The teacher shifts the focus of the classroom conversation to Rita by saying in line 55-18, "Rita, you had a comment." Rita takes the conversation back to the original question, "So what kind of a person is Dee?" (line 55-02). With her statement in line 55-21, "I think she's kind of selfish," Rita is making a claim that seems to directly connect to the teacher's original question but may also be interpreted as connected to Valerie's claim that Dee wanted to be something she wasn't. Rita's comment continues the conversation around what kind of person Dee is, provides a different perspective, and also provided an opportunity for the teacher to ask for more, or perhaps different kinds of, evidence.

The teacher continues the pattern that she established in Interactional Unit 1 of a student making a claim and the teacher subsequently asking for evidence. In line 55-22 she validates Rita's claim by saying, "OK," but then requests evidence by asking, "Why?" (line 55-23). Rita, however, makes another claim rather than giving evidence for her previous claim. Although the transcript is unclear as to the ending of Rita's comment, she begins it, "I just feel that" (line 55-25), which is an appeal to a personal privilege for presenting a claim or assertion rather than evidence. The teacher responds to Rita's new claim with "You'll learn . . . why is my favorite question" (line 55-26). She did not directly critique Rita's claim, not saying that it was right nor wrong, but instead she requests more evidence. Rita then makes an attempt to provide evidence in lines 55-27 through 55-30 when she says, "Because she wants more than she has so she's always asking to get more . . . and she's always over there just embarrassed when she shouldn't be, you know."

Line 55-31 provides a change in the conversation. The teacher does not follow the pattern that we see in the previous Interactional Unit by validating Rita's comment once evidence is given. Instead, she asked the question, "So it's a bad thing to go for what you want?" There are several reasons why the teacher may have asked this question. For example, it may be that although Rita was attempting to give evidence, the evidence that she gives for "what kind of person is Dee?" may be tied to the claim made by Valerie in line 55-05 that Dee "wants to be something she's not." It is ambiguous what claim Rita is giving evidence for. Perhaps the teacher in line 55-31 is asking Rita to be more clear about her evidence. If Rita's initial claim was related to Valerie's (if she was extending the idea that Dee wanted to be something that she wasn't and this kind of behavior is necessarily selfish) then the teacher may have been prompting Rita to give a form of evidence for her own statement that wanting more is selfish. In line 55-37 Rita does answer the question directly, saying that "you should at least share or something."

Within the context of the event and its explicit instructional task, which involved reading a text, making a claim, and providing textual evidence, Rita's comment in lines 55-27 to 55-30 could be interpreted as evidence from the text (although a careful examination of the text provides no explicit reference to Dee not sharing with her family). It could be the case that Rita has made an inference about Dee and her relationship to her family and is providing that inference as evidence. And there are other possible interpretations. What is public is that Rita has provided a response in the slot for providing evidence and the teacher publicly accepts the response as adequate, as she replies, "OK, OK" (line 55-38).

A publicly available interpretation of the teacher's question, "So it's a bad thing to go for what you want?" (line 55-31) is that she is opening the discussion up to the rest of the class and perhaps contesting the statement in lines 55-27 to 55-30. In lines 55-32 through 55-34 several students answer "no" to this question. In line 55-39 the teacher calls on Eve to share her comment. Eve's comment may have been tied to either the teacher's question in line 55-31, or it may have been tied to the teacher's initial question, "What kind of person is Dee?" (line 55-02), or it may have been connected to any of the other comments made by Eve's peers thus far in the conversation. Even so, Eve's comment in line 55-41,

"I think that it's good to go for more," is directly related to the teacher's question in line 55-31. The topic of the conversation has shifted from a direct discussion of what kind of person Dee is to whether or not it is acceptable to aspire to a different kind of life than the one from which you come.

Looking at Interactional Unit 1 within the context of Interactional Unit 2, it becomes evident that the teacher has established a pattern of asking for multiple responses to her initial question, "What kind of a person is Dee?" across Interactional Units, that is, across IRE conversational structures. By looking across the two Interactional Units, it is publicly evident that there is not one and only one correct answer to the question, but multiple possibly correct answers. The teacher has also established a pattern of soliciting claims and then asking for evidence; that is, the teacher is adapting the IRE conversational structure to provide a learning opportunity for teaching an argument structure of claim plus evidence. Such an argument structure is different from what occurred earlier in the lesson when the students were asking why they thought that people might change their names. During that segment the students were allowed to brainstorm reasons and elaborate the reasons, but did not need to provide textual evidence for their brainstormed reasons.

In analysis of Interactional Units 1 and 2, questions can be asked about what counts as a claim and what counts as evidence. In Interactional Unit 2, Rita did not provide explicit textual evidence. Her responses were similar to the responses found earlier in the lesson when the students brainstormed reasons for a name change, as Rita prefaces her response with, "I just feel that . . ." which is a bid for a different kind of argument structure, one not based on textual evidence but on respect for personal prerogative or perhaps personal experience.

The move that Rita makes in shifting the definition of what counts as argument from claim plus evidence to claim plus personal prerogative can be viewed as placing the teacher in a difficult situation because confronting Rita's response might also be a public attack on Rita's "face." It would certainly undercut Rita's bid for respect for her personal prerogative.

Just as the construction of opportunities for learning in Interactional Unit 1 required an examination of Interactional Unit 2, understanding opportunities for learning in Interactional Unit 2 requires examining Interactional Unit 3.

Interactional Unit 3 (Lines 55-39–55-60)

Interactional Unit 3 begins with the teacher asking, "Eve, what's your comment here?" (line 55-39). Eve has been waving her hand and bidding for a turn at talk during Interactional Unit 2. The teacher may have interpreted such nonverbal behavior as having a comment on Rita's argument, which is an indication of the teacher's communicative competence within this classroom community (cf. Hymes, 1974). The teacher's use of the deictic "here" suggests that the teacher is signaling to Eve and publicly giving Eve permission to comment on what has transpired in Interactional Unit 2. Eve says, "I think that it's good to go for more" (line 55-41). This is a reference to lines 55-28 and 55-29 where Rita has critiqued Dee for going for more than she has. Thereafter, the conversation in Interactional Unit 3 continues to evolve in a manner different than Interactional Units 1 and 2.

Part of what occurs in Interactional Unit 3 is that the issues that Rita raised in Interactional Unit 2 are refracted, that is, they are examined and recast. By nominating Eve for a turn at talk and allowing her to begin topic initiation in Interactional Unit 3, the teacher provides another set of learning opportunities. Through how she scaffolds the conversation in Interactional Unit 3 she models how statements may be parsed and recast in order to examine or contest an issue.

For example, Interaction Unit 3 begins with the teacher asking Eve what her comment is (line 55-39). Eve responds by taking a personal position on the teacher's previous question, responding that she thinks "it's good to go for more, but at the same time, don't make your family ashamed of you" (lines 55-41 through 55-43). This is a recasting of line 55-21 (Rita: "I think she's kind of selfish") and a response to the teacher's question in 55-31 ("So it's a bad thing to go for what you want?" and Rita's subsequent response in lines 55-34, 55-36, and 55-37). However, Eve then changes the direction of the discussion by returning to a discussion of Dee, saying, "She's not satisfied with the way she was brought up" (lines 55-47 and 55-48). It is important to note here that Eve did this without the teacher's prompting and did not wait for validation. In lines 56-49 and 56-50, Eve continues to change the pattern of conversation as she then provides evidence for her own claim about Dee. Not only does Eve provide her own evidence, but she is the first to refer back to actual events in the book for evidence (although her evidence is still based in her in- interpretations of the reading rather than on particular events that could be pointed to directly with a page and paragraph number). Further, rather that simply providing evidence and being done with her contribution, Eve draws a new conclusion about Dee: "She wants to be something different, something that excites her. Yeah" (lines 55-53 to 55-56). The teacher responds by validating her comment by repeating it (line 55-57) and saying, "That's a very good comment" (line 55-58) and then taking her own per- sonal position on Eve's comment by stating, "I like that [Eve's comment]."

Final Comments

By looking at a line-by-line analysis of Interaction Units 1 and 2, it is possible to see that a particular pattern for this discussion has been put into place by the teacher. In this classroom discus- sion, students make a claim and are then expected to give evi- dence for that claim. However, in line 55-31 the teacher asks, "So it's a bad thing to go for what you want?" This question seems to be a pivotal point in the discussion. In the analysis of Interac- tion Unit 2, there were multiple possibilities for how this message unit might have been interpreted. By sharing her personal phi- losophy about the appropriateness of "going for more," Eve is not responding directly to Rita's comment but rather to the teacher's earlier question which shifted the conversation away from claims and evidence grounded in the text. At that point, they were not talking about the text at all, but rather about their philosophies about people and how they should behave. The text became only a prop for initiating such a discussion. Eve, however, refers back to the text and begins to make claims about Dee's behavior, mak- ing inferences about how the character might feel. This is a differ- ent topic of conversation. Although Eve has returned to talking about Dee, she is not talking about what kind of person Dee is. She is talking instead about how she thinks Dee feels and con- structs her world.

Part of what is noteworthy in Eve's shifting the topic of dis- cussion in this particular classroom literacy event is not so much that Eve attempted to do this when the prerogative of the topic of conversation in classroom conversations typically rests with the teacher, but rather, the teacher's response to this shift—in other words, their acting and reacting to each other. She validates Eve's comments, going as far as to say that she liked Eve's comments. Had the teacher's response to Eve been different—for example, "Eve, that's not what we're talking about" or "Eve, can you give us a page number and a paragraph from the story to show us how you know this about Dee?"—Eve's comments would have been differently framed and set up for interpretation. Eve's message units that shifted the conversation may have then been interpreted and described as "off-task" remarks. It is key to note that none of the remarks that interrupted the pattern of discussion were coded as off task. This is because the teacher through her interactions with her students, including her reactions to their initiations, created opportunities for her students to direct, or co-direct, the flow of conversation. The learning opportunities embedded in this instructional conversation—and similarly so in all instructional conversations—depend on the flow of the conversation and on how the teacher and students react to each other, the nature of their uptake. What learning opportunities exist cannot be identified simply based on the predetermined instructional task nor on the initial conversational framing of the task. Whatever learning opportunities are established at the beginning of an instructional conversation continue to evolve and get reframed and refracted by subsequent instructional conversation.

This analysis is only a short piece of one class. In a larger study, it would be possible to look at many classes, many discussions, and many interaction units. It would be possible to examine how instructional conversations both within and across lessons created, defined, and refracted learning opportunities. Likewise, it would be possible to "re-search" these pedagogical discussions that may appear at first glance to be about topics irrelevant to classroom literacy events (such as, "Is it a bad thing to go for what you want?") or discussions that seem to wind up off topic to see what kind of learning opportunities are being created for students. The deep level of intricate, line-by-line analysis of interaction shown here is necessary to understand what happens in classrooms and how learning opportunities are created. It is necessary to examine how teachers and students react to each other, how they build on, reframe, and refract each other's comments on a message unit–by–message unit and interactional unit–by–interactional unit basis. Without such a microanalytic discourse analysis, it is possible that an observer in this class would have missed what learning opportunities were created and how they were created, and perhaps overlooked how the teacher and the students were using and interacting with written text and thus establishing a model of an academic literacy practice.

A Sociocognitive Perspective on the Discourse of Classroom Literacy Lesson

Susan R. Goldman

Researchers who take a cognitive perspective are typically interested in the way people take in, process, and represent information. All of these thinking activities reflect the interaction of the knowledge, skills, and experiences that people bring to the situation with the properties of the situation. Traditional cognitive work on learning has focused on identifying what the individual brings to the situation and what the properties of the materials and tasks in the situation are. However, many cognitive researchers, including me, have extended their lenses to examine the social and interactional properties of the situations in which people learn. This expansion of the cognitive lens explicitly recognizes that individual learning is contextualized or situated in a particular time and place, populated by one or more others.[2] Engagement with text is no exception. Traditional comprehension research has focused on individual learners interacting with text, usually a single text. However, with the advent of digital technologies, there is more emphasis on multiple texts and multiple media.

In the analysis of the classroom segment that is the focus of this chapter, I take a sociocognitive perspective and thus consider what may be happening for individual learners situated in the language arts classroom context. I am concerned with what the setting affords or makes available in the way of opportunities to learn, specifically opportunities to make meaning through critical analyses of texts. In the classroom lesson of which the focal segment is a part, there are opportunities to learn how to engage in literary analysis, how to construct meaning from a text, and how to integrate that meaning with prior knowledge and experiences whether acquired firsthand from direct experience or through text, film, or other representational media. I consider the affordances for meaning making of the materials, the purposes of the instructional activities as set forth by the teacher and taken up by the students, and of the whole-class discussion.

My sociocognitive perspective uses the discourse that occurs during the lesson as a window into the ways in which students are making sense of the tasks as put forth and explained by the teacher, the texts they are asked to read, and the text of the class discussion. In so doing, I am drawing on a theoretical and empirical knowledge base about discourse processing and text comprehension developed largely by cognitive psychologists (for discussion, see Graesser, Gernsbacher, & Goldman, 2003). I use a discourse analysis approach that relies heavily on the content of the utterances and to a lesser degree on the intonational, prosodic properties of the utterances. The approach bears a family resemblance to conversational analysis (Sacks, Schegloff, & Jefferson, 1974), differing largely in the emphasis on content and the meaning inferred from the content; intonation and prosody are used to make inferences about intended meanings of content.

Theoretical and Empirical Framework: Cognitive Perspective on Text Comprehension

In this section, I briefly introduce the theoretical constructs that guide my analysis of the classroom lesson as well as related empirical work on processes that facilitate text comprehension and understanding. The majority of these constructs and the empirical work are based on single readers reading single texts. One aspect of my work has been to extend constructs developed and validated by research with isolated, single readers to the social, interactive classroom context of multiple readers and multiple texts (Goldman, 2004; Goldman & Bloome, 2005). I use *text* to refer to print-based information as well as utterances that occur in the context of the lesson and class discussion.

A primary assumption of cognitive approaches is that understanding a text means building a mental representation of it. These mental representations are constructed through interaction with a text and have multiple layers that capture different aspects of text (Kintsch et al., 1993; Van Dijk & Kintsch, 1983). The most common layers are the surface layer, the textbase, and the situation model. The surface layer expresses the specific words, sentences, and layout of the text. The textbase captures the meaning of the text itself—what the text *says*—as expressed through the referential and intra- and intersentential relations and connections among the words in the text. The situation model is the interpretation or model of the world referred to by the text—what the reader interprets the text to *mean*. The situation model reflects the integration of prior knowledge with the information explicitly in the text. Integration processes are not willy-nilly, however. They are constrained by what is in the text and not all knowledge that might be associated with the words in the text is helpful to constructing a representation of what the text says and what it means (Coté, Goldman, & Saul, 1998; Coté & Goldman, 1999). Indeed, Coté and colleagues found that attempts to integrate associative knowledge that related to a single word, phrase, or sentence in the text but not to the overall situation model is predictive of poor learning outcomes.

Understanding a set of texts extends the layers of the representation to include how the texts relate to one another, in terms of form, meaning, and interpretation. In other words, connections across representations of multiple texts can be made among surface layers of different texts, among textbases, or among situation models. There can also be connections across different layers (e.g., textbase to situation model either within a text or across texts). Bloome and Goldman have argued that it is important to make the intertextual nature of learning from text explicit because the process of cross-connecting, especially at the situation model level (i.e., interpretive meaning) provides opportunities to deepen comprehension and learning in ways that are not typically achieved when texts are considered one at a time (Bloome & Goldman, 1999; Goldman, 2004; Goldman & Bloome, 2005).

Much of the empirical work that supports the foregoing characterization has been conducted in laboratory or laboratory-like settings in which individual learners read texts and perform some type of recall, question-answering, or problem-solving task related to the texts. From this research we know quite a bit about what kinds of processing effective learners do to understand texts. In brief, they explain to themselves what the text says and what it means, connecting information within a text and, in circumstances where multiple texts are involved, across texts. They tend to refrain from a lot of paraphrasing of sentence information. The prior knowledge associations they make tend to be relevant to the meaning and interpretation of the text. Investigations of how effective learners acquire these ways of processing text are scarce. What jumps out at me in the classroom lesson that is the focus of this chapter is that it exemplifies an instructional approach that could support the acquisition of processes that effective learners use to construct meaning and understand texts. In a whole-class discussion, the teacher leads the class through a process that I see as public construction of a textbase and situation model with clear demarcation of these processes from a general discussion that is not based on a specific text. In the remainder of my section of the chapter, I expand on this claim.

A Sociocognitive Perspective on Literary Analysis in the Ninth-Grade Classroom

The theme of the majority of the lesson is a teacher-led exploration of the question "Why do people change their names?" Students explore this question in two major phases of the lesson. First, early in the lesson they engage in a relatively unconstrained discussion in which they are free to use whatever prior knowledge they wish. They then explore the question through the construction of a public textbase for a short story, "Everyday Use" by Alice Walker, that models the academic discourse of literary analysis and evidence-based claims. Finally and still in the context of the short story, members of the class contribute to the construction of a public situation model created through the rich interpretive metaphors they offer. This progression encompasses parts of the lesson preceding the 4-minute focal segment. The focal segment itself illustrates part of the construction of the textbase and the construction of the public situation model.

It is important to consider the content and discussions that have preceded the focal segment because they constitute a shared knowledge base. That is, the teacher should be able to assume that students have access to some version of the information exchanged prior to the focal segment, including in the current lesson and in prior lessons. Within the past week, the students had read two segments from two novels about the importance and meaning of names, one segment from *Where the Heart Is* by Billie Letts (2004) and a chapter from *The House on Mango Street* titled "My Name" by Sandra Cisneros (1984). The class has discussed what's

in a name, that people often have strong feelings (liking and dis-
liking) for their names, the idea that names can convey or send a
message about the personality of an individual, and whether it is
a good idea to change your name. These discussions contribute
to prior knowledge that students might access during the focal
lesson.

The first instructional phase of the lesson (Phase 1) provides
an opportunity for some of the students to act out conversations
they have written between the main character in the "My Name"
vignette, Esperanza, and the main character in *Where the Heart Is*,
Moses. Important themes of these stories and of the conversations
that are acted out are that names can communicate something
about a person's physical or psychological characteristics, that
people often have strong feelings about their names, and that others often make fun of a person's name. After two of these have
been read, the teacher transitions to a second instructional phase
(Phase 2) with the question "Why do people change their names?"
During this phase, the teacher engaged the students in an open-
ended discussion in which students were free to offer up their
opinions, ideas, and examples. All contributions to the discussion
were validated by the teacher. This phase of the lesson provided
an opportunity for learners to reason from their prior knowledge,
using their life experiences and ideas they have gotten from other
movies or stories with which they are familiar. Phase 3 of the lesson is marked by the teacher handing out the short story "Everyday Use" for the students to read silently in class. They had approximately 20 minutes to read the six-page short story. Phase 4 of
the lesson was a whole-class discussion of "Everyday Use." In this
phase of the lesson, the teacher invoked constraints on the discussion. Goldman and Bloome (2005) described this as the transition
to the academic discourse of literary analysis: The teacher made
clear what the rules are for constructing meaning and interpretation within and across literary texts. The process is constrained—a
reader needs to understand the claims in the text and that inferences and reasoning "from" the text must be constrained by what
the text actually said. This is a constraint on reasoning that the
teacher has introduced in previous lessons. Thus the teacher invoked the academic norms for the disciplinary discourse of literary analysis: There is room for personal experiences and interpretations that bring in other literary works, but reasoning must be

based in some part of the text. That part of the text must be shared with the rest of the class. In addition, the whole-class format of the evidence-based discussion scaffolded the learning process by relying on a pooled set of resources for making meaning and creating interpretations. No one individual learner bore the entire responsibility; rather it was a shared, community-based process. It exemplifies a form of distributed cognition.

In constructing this gloss of the major instructional phases of the lesson, I am applying a sociocognitive perspective at a global level. Each phase is defined by a shift in the focal instructional activity. The second, third, and fourth phases of the lesson each speak to the question "Why do people change their names?" Phase 2 allows students to rely on what they already know. Phases 3 and 4 are based in a reading and the "rules" for reasoning and justifying an answer are clearly different from those that operated during Phase 2. An interesting issue with respect to the construction of a situation model for "Everyday Use" is whether prior knowledge elicited during Phase 2 enters into the discussion of the short story in Phase 4. Indeed, during Phase 2 students have discussed a reason people change their names that is highly relevant to understanding "Everyday Use" and name change of the main character, Dee: to distance themselves from their past and their families. One student, Valerie, refers to the main character in *Breakfast at Tiffany's.*

> 9-82 *Valerie:* sometimes you might want to change your
>   name to get rid of
> 9-83 like
> 9-84 life you had before kind of
> 9-85 like in the book
> 9-86 ummmmm
> 9-87 by James Cody Breakfast at Tiffanys
> 9-88 *Teacher:* oh yeah
> 9-89 xxxxxxxxxxxxxx
> 9-90 xxxxxxxxxxx
> 9-91 *Valerie:* and it's a umm
> 9-92 there's a girl named
> 9-93 the main character is Holly Golightly
> 9-94 and she's like a New York socialite now
> 9-95 but she used to be like a farm girl
> 9-96 her name | was Lu Lu May Golightly

9-97 and you it wouldn't like be very fashionable if your
name was like Lu Lu May
9-98 *Teacher:* ok
9-99 so it also ? . . .
9-100 *Valerie:* so to get rid of what happened before she went
to a new name

During Phase 4 the same student, Valerie, makes the connection
between Holly's purpose for changing her name and Dee's reason for doing so. What is significant from a cognitive perspective is that this one reason, of the many that were offered during
the Phase 2 discussion, is the most relevant to making sense of
the "Everyday Use" text. That it is reinstated in the context of the
Phase 4 discussion reflects an effective understanding strategy:
appropriate access and use of prior knowledge in the construction
of a situation model for the text. Thus the Phase 2 discussion got
students thinking about the many reasons people might change
their name, unconstrained by any specific text. The transition to
Phase 3 introduced a new text that was the focus of the remainder
of the lesson. In introducing the text, the teacher picked up the
same theme of why people change their names. She set the purpose for reading very explicitly:

23-77 *Teacher:* now this is a story
23-78 about
23-79 name changes
23-80 ok
23-81 and what I would like for you to do
23-82 when you are reading through this *T picks up a pen
from center table*
23-83 is look for *T may be writing on whiteboard*
23-84 the purpose of the name change
23-85 ok
23-86 and I want you
23-87 to highlight or underline
23-88 any part
23-89 anything that has to do with the purpose of the name
change
23-90 ok
23-91 the purpose of
23-92 you know

23-93 who
23-94 the individual's reasons
23-95 for changing her name
23-96 ok
23-97 the reasons
23-98 the reasons for the name change
23-99 ok
23-100 also I want you to do
23-101 want you to
23-102 mark *T is writing on the whiteboard*
23-103 the reactions
23-104 to the name change
23-105 the reactions to
23-106 I am just gonna put name change
23-107 er n c for name change
23-108 ok
23-109 so look for the reasons and the purpose
23-110 of the name change
23-111 and the reactions to the name change

In setting up the reading task, the teacher used the same language she had used earlier in Phase 2, thereby making the connection to the previous discussion. She told them the story was about
name changes. The words *purpose* or *reason* are repeated 10 times
in giving the task instructions; *reactions*, 3 times. As well, students
were told to mark places in the text where these are found. After approximately 18 minutes of silent reading, the teacher begins
Phase 4 by asking for a summary of the story. The summary provided by one student in the class, Valerie, began the creation of a
textbase representation of the story that is part of the public discourse. In the summary, Valerie brought in the same theme from
Breakfast at Tiffany's, although this is not yet connected to why Dee
has changed her name. Valerie says that Dee

45-95 *Valerie:* she doesn't want to be what they are
45-96 she doesn't want to be a xxxx farmer
45-97 she doesn't want to be a
45-98 she wants to be modern and special and everything

The public construction of a textbase proceeded as the teacher
asked for information on the lifestyle of the mother and daughter

who remained on the farm. In so doing, the teacher marks the importance of using the text, not just offering an opinion that is not tied to some evidence from the text.

45- 124 *Teacher:* someone tell me what their lifestyle is
45- 125 there are there are clues throughout the entire piece

When one student responds, "They are really close," the teacher makes explicit the need to go to the text to find parts of the text that support that inference:

45-134 *Teacher:* how do you know
45-135 *Student?:* xxxxxxxx
45-136 *Teacher:* give me give me some evidence
45-137 when I ask for evidence I want
45-138 I mean
45-139 ummmmm
45-140 give me quotes

The teacher invoked reading aloud as a way to make public this emphasis on what the text says and how it relates to the questions asked. After segments of the text were read aloud, the teacher interjected the question that motivated the read-aloud, "So what kind of life has she had?" This pattern of discourse interaction establishes a way to reason and make conclusions from the evidence in the text. The pattern occurs at least six times in the remainder of the lesson transcript. As the discussion turned to the kind of person Dee is and why she changed her name, the teacher continued this pattern. In addition to establishing a publicly available textbase representation, the pattern "question/answer/read-aloud justification from text/draw conclusion" models the discourse of literary analysis albeit at a level appropriate to the developmental range in this ninth-grade classroom.

The latter portion of this phase of the lesson is the focal segment. The beginning of the segment illustrates two examples of the emphasis on providing reasons for responses, although the insistence on reading aloud from a part of the text is implicit and not followed up. The teacher had again asked what kind of person Dee is. Valerie answered, "She wants to be something she's not" (line 55-05)

55-06   *Teacher:* ▲ <u>ok</u> she wants to be something she's <u>not</u> |
55-07   Ummmmm
55-08   because she wants nice things ↑or ↓
55-09   or |
55-10   wha- why why do you say that ↑
55-11   *Student ?:* ┌ xxxxxxxxxxxxxxxxxxxxxxxx
55-12   Valerie: └ just the way she acts she doesn't want |
        to | increased volume from V's previous utterance,
        increased speed
55-13   anybody know she likes to have |
55-14   all | house | and |
55-15   she likes to buy things that they can't afford ↓
55-16   *Teacher:* ok
55-17   *buy things they can't afford*
55-18   Rita you had a comment
55-19   *Rita:* xxxx
55-20   *Teacher:* and then we'll get
55-21   *Rita:* I think she's kind of sel+fish+
55-22   *Teacher:* ok
55-23   why ↑
55-24   *Student ?:* xxxxxxxxxxxxxxxx
55-25   *Rita:* ▼ I just feel that xxxxxx ↓ *volume decreases to
        inaudible*
55-26   *Teacher:* ▲ you'll learn why is my favorite
                     ┌ question
55-27   *Rita:* ▲ └ because she wants more than she has

The teacher asks for evidence (lines 55-10 and 55-26) although she does not insist on a read-aloud from the text, perhaps because the justifications echo points about Dee that earlier in the Phase 4 discussion were justified with parts of the text. Thus the discourse pattern for literacy analysis creates a public textbase through responses to questions that are tied to segments of the text.

The next part of the focal segment marks a transition to a more interpretive stance with respect to the text. Students begin to move to generalizations about Dee. Rita begins this process when she says she thought Dee was selfish because she wanted more than she had (line 55-27). In response the teacher invites students to reflect more generally by posing the question, "So it's a bad thing to go for what you want?" The use of *you* in the question appeared to encourage the students to bring in self-relevant knowledge and connect it with Dee, as Eve did in the following segment.

> 55-40 *Eve:* uhh
> 55-41 I think that it's goo+d to go | for more |
> 55-42 but at the same ti+me
> 55-43 don't make your family be ashamed of you+ |
> 55-44 ▼ like ummm
> 55-45 ▼ I think she wants to change herself because |
> 55-46 she | |
> 55-47 she's not satisfied with |
> 55-48 the way she | was brought up ↑ |

Eve first talks in the general case (line 55-43; *your* family ashamed of *you*) and then references Dee (line 55-45). This is the first public integration of prior knowledge with the textbase; it contributes to the construction of a publicly available situation model. In the remainder of the focal segment the interpretive level is embellished, first by Ron and then by Rachel. Ron provided a fairly well-developed metaphor of a tree.

> 55-63 *Ron:* I kinda |
> 55-64 kinda think she wants to be kinda like |
> 55-65 pretending like this her life is kinda like a tree |
> 55-66 she wants to be at the top of the tree but yet |
> 55-67 she also tries to forget the roots of it at the same time
> 55-68 so she has to keep |
> 55-69 like the roots are what made her what she is right now |
> 55-70 and if she if she didn't have the roots to support her she wouldn't have anything to actually go for
> 55-71 so she has |
> 55-72 wants to be better than her family |
> 55-73 but yet she can't forget about her family either ↓

The metaphor conveys the tension between dependence on roots but wanting to transcend those roots. In lines 55-99 to 55-100, Rachel brings to the situation model a connection with another story, "The Necklace," using it to point out the need to be realistic about your goals (lines 55-93 to 55-97). The comments of these three students used the text but moved beyond it, bringing in reasoning processes and other texts, contributing to an interpretive but publicly shared situation model. It is important to note that the interpretations are grounded in prior comments about Dee and connected to information in the text. Thus the interpretive process went beyond the text but was connected to the text.

The discourse in the different phases of this classroom lesson manifests the use of different kinds of processes and knowledge that contribute to the creation of a publicly constructed, multilayered representation that is shared by the classroom community. Each phase of the lesson invited students to participate in different forms of interaction with and about text. For example, Phase 2 emphasized reasoning based on prior knowledge and experience. Phase 4 initially emphasized reasoning closely tied to a specific text. In so doing, this phase established a publicly shared textbase that served as the agreed upon (relatively speaking) meaning of the text. It established legitimate ways to construct meaning with its emphasis on providing the evidence "from the text." The later portion of Phase 4 moved beyond the text to interpretive reasoning and contributed to the construction of a publicly shared situation model, connecting the text more directly to its "meaning in the world" and potentially to the lives of these students.

In closing, I want to return to the broader issues of engaging students with multiple texts. One goal in relating multiple literary texts is to understand relevant dimensions of comparison among the multiple texts. A second goal is to see how the themes in the literary piece are similar to and different from themes and personal experiences of the reader (Goldman & Bloome, 2005). A third goal is to learn the discourse of literary analysis, or argumentation schemes appropriate to the study of literature, whether single or multiple texts are involved. Literary interpretation, much like argumentation in other disciplines, is a constrained process: Readers need to understand the claims in the text (the textbase) and that inferences and reasoning "from" the text must be constrained by what the text actually said. To be effective comprehenders and learners, students need to master text-focused reasoning as well as interpretive reasoning that integrates relevant prior knowledge and experience with the actions, events, and human conditions portrayed in text.

The Moral Order of Questions and Answers: "What Kind Of Person Is Dee?"

Douglas Macbeth

My approach to the analysis of classroom discourse is ethnomethodological. As the study of "members' methods," ethnomethodology takes interest in how the parties to actual tasks, settings, and occasions of everyday life—including the everyday lives of classrooms—are methodically engaged in producing the order and coherence of their affairs. Among other things, these methods and practices assure the recurrence of "common understanding" (Moerman & Sacks, 1971/1988), on which every human social interaction, and institution, is leveraged, including the work of classroom order and instruction (cf. Cicourel et al., 1974; Heap, 1985; Hester & Francis, 2000; Lee, 2004; Macbeth, 1991, 2003; McHoul, 1978; Mehan, 1979; Payne & Hustler, 1980).

Ethnomethodology is also known for its insistence that we have *use* for the interactional detail of the occasions we study. It recommends local study, or the study of situated action, or social action in situ. Collecting these and other formulations, the very term ethnomethodology points to how the first analysts on the scene are not those with PhDs, but are rather ordinary social actors, in their competence to their tasks of understanding. Understanding is *itself* an analytic achievement, and turn taking may be its most vivid demonstration: To speak next (to take a turn) is to engage in the analysis of the speaking that is going on now, for what it is saying, what it is doing, what it calls for next, and most especially its projectable completion. If we cannot see what an ongoing turn is doing, and where it might end, we cannot see where to begin our own or what we might do with it. These are analytic matters, and for whatever else "common understanding" may consist of, the production of an appropriate next turn, on time, is perhaps its first and most familiar expression. To speak is to evidence our understanding of what has gone before (Moerman & Sacks, 1971/1988).

Turning to our common corpus of material, I found it a challenge to work with. Like the other contributors, I routinely work from transcript and thus the talk or discourse of the setting or occasion. For many "Discourse" has become a reductive category that collects virtually every form of human social expression (e.g., talk, texts, films, clothes, and culture). For analysts of natural conversation, however, the organizing insight is that for whatever else our distinctions, humans are a talking species. Talk, natural conversation, or talk-in-interaction is a primordial site of sociability and social action. Talk is not a representational medium, but an actionable one. It is social action's most common venue. It is how we *do* things in this world, and thus perhaps the most regular organizing question I pose when working through transcribed materials in their sequential, real-time organizations is: What—as matters of practical action, situated in the sequential implicativeness of the ongoing action that contexts it—are the parties *doing*?

It's a heuristic question. Seldom is there only one answer, yet pretty routinely some answers turn out to be more revealing than others. For example, when I reviewed the video recording of the entire 59-minute lesson, at about the 9-minute mark, the teacher has been leading the students through a discussion with an eye to their Alice Walker reading that will occur later. It has to do with people who have changed their name (as Dee has done in the reading), and why they might do that. We don't need to know what else the hour holds in order to hear that this discussion is planned and purposeful. But once we hear the entire hour, we can also hear how this discussion is showing them how to speak (and listen) when they turn to the Walker reading assignment later on. We could say they are using this discussion to prepare for a next one.

The teacher poses the question "Why do people change their names?" as part of the discussion of why someone would do that, requesting some examples. The students begin producing them. The simplified and abridged transcript below shows us something of how they do, and for now, my answer to the question, "What are students doing?" is that they are *answering*. If that seems too slight an analytic risk to hold our interest, there is some possibility that if we pursue it, it may lead us to reassess what the work of answering is in the course of a classroom, multiparty discussion: What competencies, practices, judgments, contingencies, and social organizations of answering have been taught, learned, and brought into play. Or how answering—and classroom answering especially—is far more than a correspondence exercise of cutting and measuring the contents of a question to find an answer and is instead a densely social production.

The transcript conventions used below are derived from Sacks et al. (1974). The aim is to render sequential order as it sounds. Punctuation, for example, notes intonations and associated pauses rather than grammar. Pauses are noted in seconds (e.g., 0.5). Micro pauses are noted by "(.)." Underlining shows emphasis or stress, and colons indicate a sound stretch on a word or word portion (e.g., no::). A dash indicates the cutoff of a word in its production (e.g., wha—), and a double slash (//) notes the point at which one speaker begins, overlapping another. An equal sign notes turn transition without gap or overlap. Empty brackets indicate an unheard utterance or utterance portion; filled brackets indicate an uncertain hearing. For economy of space, there is substantial ellipsis [. . .] in the transcripts. Given these conventions, the line numbering may be slightly different than in the transcripts elsewhere in the chapter.

This first transcript of a portion of the class discussion begins at the 9-minute mark.

9-1 *Teacher:* Why do people change their names. . .
9-2 *Jason:* I think they change their name [because   ]
9-3 *Teacher:* Alright. OK. Good. Rita.
9-4 *Rita:* I think that they might be hiding something.
9-5 *Teacher:*   Oh::
9-6 *Rita:*   // I mean [   ]
9-7 *Teacher:* Very good . . . that's good that's good.
9-8 *Jason,* and then we'll go to [   ].
9-9 *Student:* That is: true: because (0.5) they could like be:
9-10 hiding from tha police or somethin an: (0.5)
9-11 the police get their names so
9-12 they [   ] change their name . . .
9-13 *Teacher:* Ron, what was your comment.
9-14 *Ron:* . . . maybe some, like your na:me maybe have: like
9-15 (.) someone else might have had this name
9-16 and you kinda have like a
9-17 reputation of being what this other person ha:d cause
9-18 everyone kind of sees you as tha:t . . .
9-19 like Frankenst—the Young Frankenstine.
9-20 *Valerie:* (laughs)
9-21 *Student:* Stee:n . . .
9-22 *Teacher:* . . . So—so there cd' possibly [   ] to: (.) to
9-23 separate (0.5) yourself er—from some—some

9-24 ba:d say . . . 'oh you're just going to carry
9-25 on: the family tradition. . . like in Frankenstein's case. . .
9-26 whatever. OK good that's good Mel Brooks. . . Valerie =
9-27 *Valerie:* = OK, uhm: sometime:s you might wanna
9-28 change your name to get rid of: like (.) tha life tha' you
9-29 had before: kind 'uv?
9-30 Like in the book uhm:by James Cody Breakfast at
9-31 Tiffany's.
9-32 *Teacher:* Oh yeah . . .

One thing we can see is how these answers are built across the turns that produce them and become collaborative productions; each turn furnishes resources for subsequent turns. Rita offers the first answer we can hear: that people might change their names "because they might be hiding something." The very next student agrees, and produces a scenario of hiding—hiding from the police. Hiding is picked up by Ron as well, but here it's hiding from an association. He speaks of having the same name as another and a desire to create distance between that person and oneself. "Hiding" thus emerges from Rita's first reply about hiding something, to become a first scenario, a second one, and then the "for instance" of Young Frankenstein. And to it, Valerie offers another: the example of the female lead in *Breakfast at Tiffany's*. Each reply contexts the next, and each ties to its prior by terms that are both familiar and novel. Topic talk has an organizational life, most especially in multiparty conversation or group talk, that simply can't be accounted for by propositional contents alone, and a great many things may anchor the "tie" from one turn "on topic" to another (see Sacks, 1992).

Ways of Speaking

To further develop the methodic work of their discussion, I want to take up the teacher's first few turns in the above sequences. On first blush, the discussion throughout the hour is an open–ended one, as the teacher encourages students to contribute and receives each next contribution with appreciation. She repeatedly praises and/or thanks the students for their contributions, and thus there is every impression that this classroom discussion stands at some distance from direct instructional sequences. The classic format and expression of direct instruction is the three-turn sequence known as IRE (Initiation-Reply-Evaluation): a teacher's question is followed by a student's answer that receives an evaluation from the teacher in third turn. Mehan (1979), among others, treated this kind of organization as a sequential organization, and there is ample evidence that it is a deeply familiar modern instructional format, both in classrooms and childhood socialization. But what we find in this lesson seems quite different: There isn't likely to have been a formal curriculum that contexts the question "Why do people change their names?" Students aren't likely to have been presented with the three most common reasons for changing one's name, where such a curriculum would unavoidably be a curriculum in moral judgments. There is, however, the possibility that *this* discussion is just such a curriculum, in the service of a next one.

As some evidence of the possibility, when we look closely at the discussion at the 9-minute mark, it seems that the students are listening quite closely to the teacher's third-turn remarks (i.e., her remarks that follow directly on their answers). What we see there, at least in these first ten lines, is that the students are listening for the adequacy of their answers as expressed in whatever the teacher says next. We can see something of their orientations to the teacher's turns in lines 9-3, 9-5, and 9-7 (see transcript above).

9-1 *Teacher:* <u>Wh</u>y do people <u>c</u>hange their names . . .
9-2 *Jason:* I think they change their name [because   ]
9-3 *Teacher:* Alright. OK. <u>G</u>ood. <u>R</u>ita.
9-4 *Rita:* I think that they might be <u>h</u>iding something.
9-5 *Teacher:*   Oh::
9-6 *Rita:*   // I mean [   ]
9-7 *Teacher:* Very good . . . that's good <u>t</u>hat's good.
9-8 <u>J</u>ason, and then we'll go to [   ].
9-9 *Student:* <u>Th</u>at <u>i</u>s: true: be<u>c</u>ause (0.5) they could like be:
9-10   hiding from tha police or somethin an: (0.5)
9-11   the police get their names so
9-12   they [   ] change their name . . .

The first answer we hear is Jason's, and we can't hear all of it. Presumably a reason is given, and to it the teacher replies in line 9-2 with a graded string of rejoinders, moving upward from "Alright" to "OK" to "Good."We hear a progression where "Alright" and "OK" mark and accept the answer and are hearable for agreement and "Good" is a clearly positive assessment, though we can also observe that it's not a "very best" assessment. And if we can hear it that way we can be assured the students can too.

In the same turn, Rita is selected next [this too is hearable as part of the teacher's assessment of what interest Jason's remark holds], and Rita replies that "they might be hiding something." In the next turn we hear what Heritage (1984a) refers to as a "change of state token," or an utterance that remarks on how what has just been said has a novel register for its recipient: "Oh" is the canonical expression. Yet while it may display surprise or a piqued interest, "Oh" can be ambiguous as to just what kind of interest it shows, whether it's welcomed or not, or what it calls for next. And rather than trying to decide the question from our distance, we can note that Rita apparently hears it as calling for her to explain herself. That is, in the next turn and beginning in overlap, she clarifies, adumbrates, or repairs her reply. We can't hear how she does so; we can only hear her preface, "I mean. . . ." And then, for whatever Rita says next, we have in line 9-7 the teacher's clearly upgraded appreciation "very good," upgraded further in the redundancy of "that's good that's good."

Though Jason seems to be called upon next, a different student speaks, and I only want to note the topical continuity from Rita's turn to this one: The student begins with an agreement ("That is true . . .") and proceeds to offer a concrete scenario of hiding. In doing so she's speaking on a topic that has already been marked and assessed as very good. It's tempting to say that her answer thus displays both a topical good sense, and a local organizational good sense. But we can describe it that way only if we can clearly see a difference between the two, between the topical and the organizational. When we look, however, we find that the local order of answering is a constant companion to every propositional or content formulation we make, and that the distinction between content and production is difficult to sustain. Answers are local productions.

Though at first the discussion looks nothing like the canonical IRE organization of questions with known answers, further consideration shows that the students are clearly oriented to the teacher's remarks in next turn to student replies, and were we working on the entire hour's transcript, we would see this throughout. On the other hand, however, notwithstanding some failed understandings and reexplanations, the teacher never *doesn't* accept a student's reply or answer. No one is ever sent back to think about it further, and every reply is well received. We could say that every turn by the teacher that follows on a contribution by a student is a positive one. But also in every case, the students are attuned to a certain economy of praise, and all praise is not equal.

The target sequence occurs at minute 55. It's contexted by everything that has gone before, including the introduction and distribution of the Walker reading at the 21:58-minute mark, followed by a silent reading. Both before and then after the reading, further instruction is offered about just what they are to do with the reading, or how they are to discuss it. The following sequence is prior to the reading, and there is substantial ellipsis. This transcript begins at minute 23:41.

23-1 Now this is a story, about name: changes (1.0) OK.
23-2 And what I would like fer' you to do: (0.7) when you
23-3 are reading through this (1.0)
23-4 is look for the purpose of the name change, OK?
23-5 And I want you: (.) to high:light: or underline: any
23-6 part, anything that has to do:
23-7 with the purpose of the name change, OK?. . .
23-8 The purpose of: f—you know who the individual's
23-9 rea:sons for changing her name, OK . . .
23-10 Also I want you to do: want you to mark the reactions
23-11 (.) to the name change . . . So look for the
23-12 reasons and the purpose (.) of the name
23-13 change and the reactions to the name change . . .
23-14 *Student:* Read it silently?
23-15 *Teacher:* Yes, read it silently . . .

We, and the students, can hear the open parameters of their prior discussion narrow a bit, as the teacher tells them in advance what they might be looking for in the reading and how they might organize any account they then make of it. Her instructions are a virtual announcement of the topics for their reading and how to address them.

There is similar instruction to be heard as the postreading discussion begins. The teacher announces that she'll be expecting their answers to her various questions about the story to be accompanied by "evidence," and that the best evidence will be actual quotations from the reading. She asks the students to summarize and formulate the life styles of the protagonists, what clues they have for their accounts of life style, what images they find of the mother and of the very different relationships she has with her two daughters. As we come to the targeted sequence, the question is about Dee, the older daughter, who has left home, gone to college, and embraced a world of fashion, an identity and ambition that appears to some students to set her apart from her upbringing. She returns home for a brief visit with a new, Africanized name, a request for a family heirloom, and a man. This is the tale that contexts the question "What kind of person is Dee?"

The delicacy of the question is evident: It is unavoidably a moral question, a question of character, of "kinds" of persons. Again, I mean *moral* in the peculiar way in which every account or description has the horizon of a moral world attached, although as it develops, the ensuing discussion takes up this task of moral speaking quite explicitly, and becomes moral in a more familiar vein. Further, and for that reason (that the discussion calls for moral judgment), it proceeds in a way that has no particular need for the Walker text to clarify the moral probities involved. Morality is after all a universalist discourse; it is a principled way of speaking, and the lesson becomes a matter of organizing and reconciling a moral discourse in such a way that unequivocal condemnation is very hard to come by.

The segment begins at the 55:25-minute mark with the question, "So what kind of person is Dee?" After an exchange of turns with Valerie about how Dee wants things her family can't afford, the teacher selects Rita:

55-21 *Rita:* I̲ think she's kinda sel:fish: =
55-22 *Teacher:* = OK̲.
55-23 W̲hy.
55-24 *Student:* (She always good lookin'.)
55-25 *Rita:* I jus:: (.) ( ) (1.0)
55-26 *Teacher:* Wha– y̲ou learn̲ed that w̲hy is my f̲avorite
55-27 question.
55-28 *Rita:* / / ( ) –   / / Bec̲ause she w̲an:ts uhm,

55-29 <u>m</u>ore:: than she has:, an' she's always <u>a</u>f:ter (tryin' ta'
55-30 get) more. . . and (   ) she's always <u>o</u>ver there
55-31 there just (.hh) em<u>bar</u>:rassed when she
55-32 shouldn't be ya' know (   )?
55-33 *Teacher:* So it's a <u>bad</u> <u>thing</u> ta' go: fer what you <u>w</u>ant?
55-34 *Valerie:* No. (1.0)
55-35 *Student:* No. =
55-36 *Rita:*   = No:: ((rising inflection))
55-37 *Teacher:*   / / I'm playin <u>d</u>evil's advocate here.
55-38 *Rita:*   / / <u>Y</u>ou <u>sh</u>ouldn't be em<u>bar</u>:rassed
55-39 if (.) yer family lives like
55-40 that an– or <u>n</u>o:t, ya' know:?, you shd' be at <u>l</u>east
55-41 <u>sh</u>a:ring or something.
55-42 *Teacher:* O<u>K</u>. OK.
55-43 Eve <u>w</u>hat's your comment here. . .

In the interest of space, I want to organize the discussion of the sequence (lines 55-21 through 55-43) with a direct question for the reader as a competent hearer of classroom discourse about the teacher's question in line 55-33:

55-33 *Teacher:* So it's a <u>bad</u> <u>thing</u> ta' go: fer what you want?

My question is: Is the teacher's turn of line 33 a question with a known answer? It's clearly a yes or no question, but in hearing the question, do we hear a preference for one of them? That is, does the teacher have an answer in mind, and, if she does, which is it?

The questions remind us that in the analysis of naturally oc-curring discourse, *our* (the professional analyst's) cultural compe-tence to 'how we talk and listen' is the central analytic resource. The answers to the above questions require no further credentials. I have quizzed a handful of people about the teacher's question and my questions about it, and to a person their answers have been "Yes, the question the teacher asks projects, in the asking, an answer," and the answer it projects is "No, it's *not* a bad thing to go for what you want." Further, the students give ample evi-dence of the same answers in their succeeding turns: More than one student answers no, including Rita to whom the question is posed. There is something evident about the answer to the teach-er's question for them too. But these are the easy questions and answers for our account. The tough ones, the analytic questions, are to understand by what resources in the sequential production of the discourse, in its particulars, a competent interlocutor is so instructed to hear the teacher's question in these ways.

My answers to the tough questions are not certain. But they begin with the regular way in which the teacher has been producing her 3rd-turn remarks in the lesson (her remarks in next turn to student replies and contributions). As in the prior sequence, by and large she marks them with an accepting receipt, often done with "OK"s or "Good," and also by repeating or "formulating" what the student has just said. The difference between a repeat and a formulation is fairly straightforward: a *formulation* says the same in different words, or by ellipsis, or offers a gist (Garfinkel & Sacks, 1970). The teacher's line 55–33 is such a thing, made of Rita's reply.

Rita, in line 55-21, has offered a straightforward character assessment of Dee: "I think she's kind of selfish." The teacher accepts with an "OK" and asks "why?" and following intervening talk, Rita re-begins with what turns out to be a three-part answer (lines 55-28 to 55-33). She offers three "why" accounts in support of her "selfish" assessment, and it is this turn that the teacher formulates as a gist or upshot in the question "So it's a bad thing to go for what you want?" (line 55-33).

> 55-26 *Teacher*: Wha– you learned that why is my favorite
> 55-27 question.
> 55-28 *Rita*: // (   ) –   // Because she wan:ts uhm,
> 55-29 more:: than she has:, an' she's always af:ter (tryin' ta'
> 55-30   get) more. . . and (   ) she's always over there
> 55-31 there just (.hh) embar:rassed when she
> 55-32 shouldn't be ya' know (   )?
> 55-33 *Teacher*: So it's a bad thing ta' go: fer what you want?
> 55-34 *Valerie*: No. (1.0)
> 55-35 *Student*: No. =
> 55-36 *Rita*:   = No:: ((rising inflection))
> 55-37 *Teacher*:   // I'm playin devil's advocate here.

We can note this much about the work the teacher has done on Rita's prior turn: Of the three characterizations Rita has made, the teacher picks up on only one of them, that Dee "wants more than she has." It's formulated as the question of line 55-33, presumably for Rita to answer, and yet others respond to it too, and in some way, it's heard as a question for all, or at least all who have weighed in on the question "What kind of person is Dee?" Valerie answers first, and it was indeed Valerie who spoke the first critique of Dee as someone who "wants to be something she's not" (line 55-05).

Note further that while we can say the question calls for an answer of yes or no, in full it calls for agreement or disagreement. These are usefully different things. We can say the former are relevant to a propositional discourse; the latter, to an interactional one. Further still, the teacher's question is calling for agreement to a formulation that Rita has not produced. It is the teacher's gist of Rita's reply that is the object of agreement or disagreement. Thus one can reply to the question without agreeing or disagreeing with Rita. And for the very same reason, the students can reply without agreeing or disagreeing with the teacher: Though she has produced a gist, it's of another's position, not her own position. Nor need the students agree or disagree with the contents of the teacher's question; they can instead respond to the issue of whether it faithfully stands on behalf of what Rita has said—whether or not it is an apt or fair or agreeable upshot of Rita's account. Indeed, pending an uptake, no one owns the position expressed in the question. Instead, and methodically, it has been produced as a curious kind of orphan. As the teacher remarks in line 55-37, "I'm playing devil's advocate here," and this too is a piece of instruction for hearing the question—that it is a rhetorical question, or one to which the teacher has no actual commitment. It is no one's question in just these ways. Its ownership is attenuated, and in the absence of an owner, the interactional valence of disagreement is attenuated too. These organizational production features work as a virtual invitation to disagree with the gist question, and we have further still the play of equivalencies found in the question itself: To answer yes is to affirm an equivalence between "going for what one wants"—a familiar trope in our consumer culture of self–possession—and "bad things." On those grounds too, disagreement seems to become the unmarked answer and agreement the marked one. As the "known answer," "no" is relieved of its disagreeableness.

From the vantage of sequential analysis, "markedness" (Levinson, 1983) has to do with what is called preference organization, or how, in the presence of a turn that shows alternative actions in next turn (to agree or disagree with an assessment, to accept or decline an offer or invitation, and so on), there is a structural preference for a particular alternative (e.g., agreement). This preference has nothing to do with what anyone would prefer but rather is a structural regularity observed in natural conversation. Preferred next turns are typically produced on time; dispreferred next turns are produced with some kind of delay, qualification, or temporizing.

The students reply in three ways to "So it's a bad thing to go for what you want?" The first reply is a sequence of No's, the first of which is Valerie's and arrives on time or within a normal intraturn duration [line 55-34]. There is a one-second pause and we hear a second "No," to which Rita latches her stretched "No" in line 55-36. The hearing leaves the impression that the first two replies are responding to the formulation per se, while Rita's is assessing whether the gist has been a fair one of her prior turn. She continues by turning to a different feature of her account. Whereas the teacher pulled her remark about "wanting more" into relief, Rita returns to the moral probities of "being embarrassed" about one's family, a feature of her account that the teacher left without remark. The teacher accepts her rejoinder in line 55-42 and selects others to comment further.

It is these other students, first Eve and then Ron and then Rachel, who directly address the tension that organizes the teacher's gist question: the moral register of "going for what you want." They do so in a consistent manner. Each produces a balanced claim between the desires of the individual and the responsibilities of family. Eve says,

> 55-44 *Eve:* I think tha:t (.) it's goo:d ta' go: (.) for mo:re (1.0)
> 55-45 bu:t (.) at the sa:me ti:me (.)
> 55-46 don't make your (.) family be ah'shamed of you: (1.0)

Ron offers the metaphor of one who is entitled to strive for the treetops, but only on condition that she not forget her roots (lines 55-63 to 55-73). And Rachel affirms the entitlement to "go after your goals," but makes the distinction between goals and "fantasies" (lines 55-92 to 55-100). Each of these students thus produces a nuanced account of the equities implicit to the teacher's question in line 55-33, and each shows that a thoughtful account of the teacher's prior question, "What kind of person is Dee?" will not admit the moral simplicities implicit to her question (and by implication, implicit to the direction of Rita's and Valerie's remarks). They have heard *how* the teacher is speaking in line 55-33 (as "devil's advocates" do), and found instruction in *what kind* of speaking is called for next. As for how they are speaking, note finally that as it develops, there are no relevant evidences from the reading. The discussion the teacher's question mobilizes isn't one to be settled by consulting the text. For the duration of the discussion, the curriculum here is one of how we speak, or how we assess, or how we take the measure of others, and how we do so with something like restraint, balance, and a thoughtful evenhandedness. These adjectives are of course deeply moral matters, and in just this way their curriculum has become a moral curriculum. Reflexively, in their moral assessments of others, the students constitute themselves as moral actors (or as persons who speak philosophically or metaphorically) who are practicing a register of assessment for acting that way.

Final Comments

Assuming this has been at least a recognizable account of the target sequence, I have two further remarks about these materials. The first returns to an earlier observation about how we—those who publish analyses of discourses—are not the first analysts on the scene. In classrooms the force of the observation is to remind us that classroom instruction is a sustained analytic and instructional spectacle. For all those who are not speaking now, the spectacle is afforded in their analyses of those who are speaking: how their speaking is organized, how every next turn ties to its prior and projects a sequential horizon of actionable possibilities for subsequent turns, and how these possibilities are realized. These are instructive matters. Eve, Ron, Rachel, and the rest have been witness to and analysts of how the teacher has been speaking, how others have been speaking, what sense has been made of her question, what sense she has made of what sense has been made, and so forth. Their analyses entail a reading of projectable interactional organizations. We can say in the most serious sense that they are studying the teacher, and their classmates, and their productions-in-concert of the local sense and meaning of their lesson, through their talk-in-interaction. That they now see how the teacher has been speaking and find in these local spectacles how they might be speaking is the familiar, though largely unacknowledged, work of classroom instruction. It is how knowledge, competence, and their practice are organized and installed in the room, in full and public view, as they must be if you would teach novices a curriculum they do not know (Macbeth, 2000). To imagine otherwise, or to disdain "reading the teacher," is to subscribe to a rank form of naive induction, as though students plucked their instruction from feral fields of knowledge. They do not. They are instructed, and describing and understanding how they are instructed may be a useful task for the research literature.

My second remark asks this question: Is the target sequence serving an instructional purpose, is the teacher acquitting her instructional responsibilities over its course (without which we can't quite hold the students responsible for theirs), and can we assess these things? I ask it in part because so much of the contemporary literature seems oriented to this question—and intends to have an answer for it, yes or no—as though we were entitled to answers and any and every next sequence of classroom life were accountable to the question. I doubt that is so. I doubt that every interactional sequence within a lesson period is so available or accountable.

Yet I do think this teacher is offering an admirable curriculum in temperate moralizing. That's a delicate point—and phrase. Via other devices of discourse, there are very powerful social forces at play who, on seeing that there might be moral instruction of any kind at work in classrooms, are prepared to demand that it be of a kind that they approve. They would use the term *moral* as though to find it at all were to authorize their peculiar version. But the moralizing we see here is of a different kind. It is the unavoidable moral register of everyday life, revealed in how we speak of others, measure relationships, and assess ambitions, desires, and civilities. Literature can fix these things for us, at least long enough to catch a glimpse of them in other lives first, and then perhaps in our own.

It's a nice question how on earth we would ever teach such things. The analysis of naturally occurring classroom discourse can offer some instruction in that regard, but with the understanding that the curriculum we have just witnessed owes nothing in particular to the powers of formal curricular designs or distinctions. There is, of course, a formal curriculum here as well, on analyzing literature. Our target sequence is a small piece of this larger task and shows its own curriculum. As for the relationship between the formal one and this local enactment, it is praxiological. In the sequence we see how formal curricula are enacted; we see how the teacher works to show the students how to think and talk about Dee, by indirection. Yet that she instructs is unavoidable. In places like these we're reminded, as Dewey (1904) reminded us, of the great continuity between classroom instruction and pedagogies of everyday life. A foundational instructional technology—the systematics of ordinary talk-in-interaction—underwrites them both, and within these pedagogies for novices, and notwithstanding a now-conventional wisdom to the contrary, questions with known answers show themselves as delicate, complex, and instructive organizational things.

"What Kind of Person is Dee?": Interrogating Black Female Identity in Alice Walker's "Everyday Use"

Stephanie Power Carter

Collins (2000) defines Black Feminist thought as "those experiences and ideas shared by African American women that provide a unique angle of vision on self, community, and society—and theories that interpret these experiences" (p. 3). She views Black Feminist thought as "specialized knowledge" created by African American women that articulates a stance, which includes theoretical interpretations of Black women's realities by those who live it. Black Feminist theory has made contributions by examining how Black women have been historically portrayed and constructed and by making visible how Black female identity has often been obscured and misunderstood in larger society. Collins argues that maintaining the invisibility of Black women and their ideas has helped to construct negative relations of race, gender, class, and inequality that have come to pervade our nation's entire social structure. These constructions have exploited Black femaleness and attempted to characterize Black women in particular ways (e.g., faithful and obedient domestic servants, matriarchs, overly aggressive women, unfeminine women) that do not capture the complexities of their cultural epistemologies and experiences. Although a white-male-dominated society constantly attempts to characterize Black women in negative ways, Black Feminists suggest that because Black women have a distinct view of the contradictions between the dominant group's actions and ideologies and their own experiences that they have been able to develop distinct epistemologies that are in direct contrast to those of dominant society. These epistemological understandings are complex. Black Feminists argue that although Black women may have different ways of interpreting and understanding the world, society is still dominated by European male-centered epistemologies; thus educating others is made more difficult. Lorde (1984) notes that "it is axiomatic that if [Black women] do not define ourselves for ourselves, we will be defined by others—for their use—and to our detriment" (p. 45).

I use a Black Feminist lens to examine how Black female identity is positioned and contested in the classroom discussion in the target event, which focused on Alice Walker's short story, "Everyday Use" (1973; text cites refer to this source) in which an educated African American female, Dee, returns home. A Black Feminist frame is useful when examining such a discussion because it helps make visible hidden ideological stances that position Black female identity negatively. Moreover, a Black Feminist lens forces us to raise questions such as the following:

- What are the various ways in which African American female identity is portrayed within students' comments?
- What textual evidence supports their interpretations and portrayal of Dee?

Furthermore, a Black Feminist lens helps provide and make visible possible alternative interpretations to the discussion and also helps to contextualize this classroom discussion in a broader context as a means to make visible ideological stances that attempt to negatively interpret and define Black female identity. In my analysis and discussion of this classroom event, I combine a Black Feminist theory frame with a microethnographic approach to discourse analysis (cf. Bloome et al., 2005). Microethnographic discourse analysis focuses on uses of language and other means of communications as people interact with each other to construct an event while also emphasizing social and cultural processes.

I began by making my own transcript of the videotape data and creating a line-by-line description of implicit and explicit references to Walker's character Dee (e.g., line 55-21 Rita's comment "I think she's kind of sel+fish"). In my analysis of these references, I considered how students and the teacher described Dee and how students' and the teacher's interpretations about Dee were substantiated or not with Walker's "Everyday Use." I highlight two findings from my analysis:

- Student interpretations about Dee, a Black female character are not supported in the text, but these interpretations are seldom challenged in the classroom context.
- Student comments represent larger ideological stances that negatively position African American female identity.

The first of these findings is evident despite the call by the teacher for textual support for student claims. The second of these findings is evident materially and is not just a matter of interpretation. That is, there is material evidence in what the teacher and students did and did not do that connects their comments to larger ideologies about African American female identity. It is the combination of Black Feminist theory and microethnographic discourse analysis that makes the two findings visible and material. I present these findings here in a narrative retelling of the event.

In line 55-02, the teacher poses the question, "What kind of person is Dee?" In doing so, the teacher raises questions about Dee's personhood. Egan-Robertson (1998) defines *personhood* as a dynamic and cultural construct about who is and what is considered a person, what attributes and rights are constructed as inherent to being a person, and what social positions are available within the construct of being a person" (p. 453). Bloome et al. (2005) also offer ideas on personhood:

> Personhood includes shared assumptions about the characteristics and attributes that are assumed to be inherent in a person. Thus how a cultural group defines person has broad implications

and is intimately connected to issues of morality, social structure, social interaction. . . . The shared concept of personhood held by a group is part of the process of assigning meaning and significance and structuring social order. (p. 3)

Personhood is a central issue in Black Feminist theory both as a historic dimension and as part of a cultural critique. It is not just that there are negative representations of Black women, but historically Black women have been denied personhood (as enslaved people they were not defined as human) and in contemporary representations in the mass media they are positioned as second-class citizens (e.g., ancillary to others as maids, sexual objects, and so on). When using personhood as a lens, the teacher's question is significant because it asks students to discuss Dee as a person and raises the issue of who Dee is, who or what kind of person Dee represents. Another interpretation of the teacher's question might be: What kind of person is this African American female character Dee? What kind of people are African American females? Although the teacher never specifically articulates the later interpretation, what plays out in the classroom discussion via student comments about Dee suggests that students are not only discussing Dee's character as described in the text but that they began to articulate interpretations that mirror larger societal stereotypes about Black females in general.

For example, a white female student, Valerie, is the first to respond to the teacher's question. She asserts that, "Dee wants to be something that she is not" (line 55-05). Valerie's response again raises the question, Who is Dee? Perhaps her statement that Dee wants to be something that she is not is in reference to Dee's name change. The text notes that upon Dee's arrival home she informs her mother that she no longer uses her birth name, Dee:

> '"No, mama, she says". "Not Dee, Wangero Leewanika Kemanjo!" "What happened to Dee?" I wanted to know. "She's dead", Wangero said. "I couldn't bear it any longer being named after the people who oppress me."(p. 9)

Although one can see how changing her name might be interpreted as trying to change who she is, it is not clear that changing from an Americanized name to a more Afrocentric name means that "she wants to be something that she is not." (One might argue that the name change to Wangero is more symbolic of who Dee truly is/wants to be and her effort to reconnect with her African heritage. Although Dee has an Afrocentric sounding name, it is not an African name. Hoel (n.d.) proposes that Walker purposefully misspelled the names to illustrate the complexities of African American identity in America. Wanjiru is a Kikuyu name, and one of the other original nine clan names of the Kikuyus. Leewanika, who was a King in Zambia from 1842–1916, is a Malawi name. Kamenju is a Kikuyu name as well. All of the names are from the East African region and misspelled in the text.) Contrasting this alternative interpretation of Dee's name change with the interpretation that Valerie provided helps make visible an ideological stance that assumes that African American females who seek to reconnect with their cultural heritage and disconnect from dominant Eurocentric culture are suspect and/or phony. Naming and defining one's self has been central to Black Feminist epistemologies (Collins, 2000) as well as Black culture. (Karenga, 2005).

Earlier in the lesson the students had brainstormed possible reasons as to why people might change their names, but in this discussion students do not explicitly discuss naming. It is also the case that the Valerie does not directly use naming to support her stance. Valerie continues to support her assertion about Dee being "something she is not" (line 55-05) and states "she wants nice things" (line 55-08). In the text, Dee's mother states: "Dee wanted nice things. . . . She was determined to stare down any disaster in her efforts." Although the student does not directly answer the question of who Dee is, she indirectly answers the question by addressing who she is not. What is problematic is that the student's interpretation of Dee wanting "nice things" (lines 55-13 and 55-14) positions Dee negatively, whereas in the text, Dee's mother associates Dee wanting nice things with her strong determination to persevere. Valerie's interpretation suggests that Dee wanting nice things makes Dee someone she is not, hence African American females who change their names and want nice things are trying to be something that they are not.

The teacher tries to problematize Valerie's comment by asking her to clarify her statement (line 55-10: "Why do you say that"). The student continues "she likes to buy things they can't afford" (line 55-15). At no point in the text do we see Dee buying things that she can't afford. The text notes that prior to her name change she "hated the house that burned and that she made a green suit from an old suit that someone gave her mother." The story does not mention Dee's debt. In fact, no money is exchanged, and we see Dee asking her mother for family treasures that cannot be purchased but must be given. Again, the student's interpretation of Dee as buying things that she cannot afford is problematic. The student's interpretation raises the question of who Dee has come to represent and what ideological stances are at play in constructing such an interpretation without textual evidence even though the teacher had originally demanded that student comments be supported by textual evidence.

Valerie's interpretation and representation goes unchallenged by the teacher or by other students. In line 55-17 the teacher repeats Valerie's comment. At that point the teacher has a choice. She can extend the discussion and directly or indirectly challenge the basis on which Valerie has made the claim about who Dee is or she can end the interaction with Valerie and move on to another interaction. She chooses the latter. The teacher may have had many reasons for doing so—the need to get other students involved in the instructional conversation, a desire to get to other topics, and so forth. At issue is not what was in the teacher's mind, but what was constructed regardless of what was in the teacher's mind or the minds of any individual student. What was publicly constructed through the instructional conversation was a representation of Dee, an African American female character, that negatively positioned her without direct textual evidence despite a call for such evidence. Valerie's interpretation of the text in juxtaposition with the actual text suggests that Dee is also a representation of Blackness and Black femaleness that exists within the larger society (Collins, 2000; Wade-Gayles, 1997; hooks, 1993).

The teacher moves from Valerie and asks Rita, a Black female student, to answer her question. Rita states, "I think [Dee's] kind of selfish" (line 55-21). The teacher asks her, "Why?" (55-23). Rita continues, "Because she wants more" (line 55-27). The student suggests that Dee is selfish because she wants more. It is not clear if the student makes this assertion based on Dee asking her mother for family treasures, in particular the quilts that her mother had promised to her sister. The student continues, "She's always over there embarrassed when she shouldn't be you know" (55-29 to 55-30). She does not directly describe why Dee is always embarrassed; however, one might infer that she arrives at this point based on the text's description of the house: "It is three rooms just like the one that burned, except the roof is tin; they don't make shingle roofs anymore. There are no real windows, just some holes cut in the sides." Yet, the text never mentions that Dee is embarrassed. Instead, Dee's mother states that "[Dee] wrote me once that no matter where we choose to live, she will manage to come see us." Also early on in the text, Dee's mother describes Dee's sister Maggie as "ashamed" and she states that Maggie will stand hopelessly in corners—homely and ashamed. Rita's use of "should not" suggests that Dee is morally inept because she leaves her family in a three-room house with no windows and does not "share" her nice things. The use of *should* (line 55-30) infers what is just and right and that being "always embarrassed," is not "right." Further, the student appears to interpret Dee's education and upward mobility in negative ways, instead of viewing Dee's upward mobility as progress, her mother's struggles as sacrifice, and her sister's stagnation as fear. Viewing Dee's upward mobility or her "wanting to be more" in negative ways assumes that Dee's mother and sister are not content with who they are and positions them as victims. This subsequently suggests that Dee is in part responsible for their predicament. Dee's embarrassment is not supported in the text; instead, the story ends with Maggie and her mother just sitting in the yard "enjoying until it was time to go to bed."

Although the teacher attempts to problematize Rita's earlier comment and ask if it is a bad thing to want more, Rita responds, "No, but you should not be embarrassed if your family is not like you—you should at least share" (55-36 to 55-37). This statement again, portrays Dee as selfish, stingy, and embarrassed, and positions her mother and sister as helpless and hopeless. By doing so, it makes Dee appear responsible for their poverty-stricken lifestyle.

The teacher then calls on Eve (55-39), another African American female. Eve does not refer to Dee's character right away but gives an opinion, "I think that it is good to go for more" (55-41). Eve appears to be contesting Rita's statement, which suggests that Dee's upward mobility is negative. Moreover, her initial comments represent a shift from the text. She articulates a belief statement that provides a unique perspective that helps to reposition Dee in a more positive way. Eve also flips the use of "ashamed." Instead of Dee being ashamed, she states. "Don't make your family be ashamed of you" (55-43). By doing so, she acknowledges that

Dee's family has agency and that they too can be embarrassed. Eve continues that she believes that Dee wants to change herself because she was not satisfied with the way she was brought up (55-45 to 55-55). Eve's comments do not villanize Dee in the way that her peers' comments do. Eve completely repositions and views Dee's upward mobility or need for change as self-motivation or exciting. Eve's interpretation of Dee is the only alternative interpretation in the classroom discussion that does not view Dee negatively.

A white male student, Ron, speaks metaphorically and describes Dee as "pretending" and likens Dee's experiences to a tree with roots, discussing how disconnected Dee is to her family (lines 55-63 to 55-73). His comments are not taken up by his peers; instead, a white female student, Rachel, responds to Eve's earlier comment. She states, "There is nothing wrong with going after your goals but going after 'fantasies' is a whole different thing. . . ." (55-93 to 55-94). This comment suggests that what Dee is trying to achieve is unattainable and unrealistic.

Who is Dee? By the end of the classroom discussion, Dee, who is described as an educated African American woman has been publicly positioned as a phony, because she wants nice things, and selfish, because she always wants more, wants to buys things that she cannot afford, and tries to disconnect from her family. Only once during the discussion did a student attempt to view Dee in a semipositive light by suggesting that it was OK for Dee to want more. Part of what is problematic is that the statements about Dee's character are not supported by the text. The students are unable to see the possibilities and strengths of the characters— their ability to persevere. Washington (1994) argues that "all three women characters are artists: Mama, as the narrator, tells her own story; Maggie is the quilt maker, the creator of art for 'everyday use'; Dee, the photographer and collector of art, has designed her jewelry, dress and hair so deliberately and self-consciously that she appears in the story as a self-creation" (p. 101). Black Feminists would argue that the students are unable to see the strength of Dee's character because there is a larger societal discourse on African American women that seeks to construct them negatively (Collins, 2000; Higginbotham, 1992). This negative construction of African American women, when unexamined, has real consequences for all students and can be psychologically and academically damaging to African American females (Ladner, 1972).

Applying a Black Feminist's analysis illustrates the need for researchers to use multiple epistemological understandings as they attempt to interpret and understand the experiences of others, particularly those from historically marginalized groups. It also illustrates how important it is for researchers to interrogate and critique their own and each other's understandings of people they research; otherwise, educational researchers run the risk of positioning certain groups negatively. More important, just as some students in the discussion missed an opportunity to revision Dee's experiences, as educational researchers we can also miss opportunities to revision the people we study in more positive ways. Our characters are real people, and our interpretations can have huge consequences and implications for their lived experiences in educational contexts and in the larger society. Examining "who" in research not only involves the people who are being studied but also the people who study them.

Notes

1. Triangulation refers to obtaining the perspectives of the teacher and students to assess the degree to which each concurs with the researcher's interpretation of what happened in the event and what the shared, interactional meaning of any behavior or set of behaviors was. Triangulation is one method for seeking internal validity regarding an emic or grounded description.

2. Even when no "others" are physically present, there are social aspects to learning that arise due to the role of others in creating the materials and tasks in which learners engage. As well, learners may have interacted previously with others about the learning materials and tasks or may be remembering what others have said or done in connection particular learning topics.

CHAPTER 4

Laminating Discourse Analyses of Language and Literacy Events in Classrooms

How any research study *matters*—that is, how it contributes to building a knowledge base, increasing theoretical insights and framings, and addressing the "problems" people experience in their daily lives—has been undertheorized. The default assumption appears to be that bits of knowledge either add to the extant research knowledge base or create dissonance with previous findings that may require rethinking theoretical constructs. Yet, as debates about how to synthesize research findings suggest (e.g., Coffey & Atkinson, 1996; Cooper, 1982; Noblit & Hare, 1988; Wolf, 1986), assumptions about research findings being additive are questionable. It is not just that all research studies have flaws and limitations or, as poststructuralist scholars have suggested, that all research studies are partial and conducted from a "position" and within an "ideology" (e.g., Gitlin, 1994; Kaomea, 2003; Kumashiro, 2001), but rather that there has been a general failure to theorize the relationships among research studies. It often seems as if research studies are viewed as if they are things not of this world rather than as events themselves located in time, in particular settings, and with particular people. If the knowledge derived from a research study is not viewed as abstract or idealized but as inherently connected to the contexts and particularities of the events of its derivation, then the process of building knowledge across studies is similar to the social processes involved in connecting any set of social events, what Floriani (1993) labels *intercontextuality*. In brief, the process of building knowledge across research studies is one of social construction and rhetorical processes.

Bloome et al. (2005) suggest that there are four kinds of relationships among research studies: complementary, parallel, null set, and antagonistic. *Complementary relationships* refer to compatibility with regard to the underlying theoretical assumptions about language, people, and knowledge. *Parallel relationships* refer to the use of similar dimensions or aspects but not necessarily complementarity of underlying theoretical assumptions; the presentation of the four approaches to discourse analysis in Chapter 3 is an example of parallel relationships. *Null set relationships* refer to relationships among research perspectives that appear on the surface to have some relationship to each other, but upon deeper inspection are not at all about the same thing. For example, two studies of classroom reading instruction may both be labeled discourse analysis studies but their definitions of discourse and their definitions of reading may be so different that they are not at all studying the same thing nor using similar approaches. *Antagonistic relationships* refer to mutually exclusive theoretical constructs across research perspectives.

In this concluding chapter, we begin by noting four themes in approaching discourse analysis studies that we have emphasized throughout the book. Taken together, these four themes characterize discourse analysis studies as dialectical practice, as creating productive tensions that yield new insights and ways of understanding language and literacy events in classrooms. After discussing the four themes and how the contribution of findings from discourse analysis studies of language and literacy events in classroom might be conceptualized, we discuss how multiple discourse analysis studies might be brought together, a process we call *laminating*. A lamination bonds together a series of layers in such a way that each remains recognizable but together may be stronger and put to new uses. At issue in any lamination is what constitutes the different layers and what bonds them together as well as and how the use for which the lamination is intended influences the layers and how they are connected.

DISCOURSE ANALYSIS AS DIALECTICAL PRACTICE

We have emphasized four themes in approaching discourse analysis studies of language and literacy events in classrooms. First, there are many definitions of discourse and multiple approaches to discourse analysis. Second, knowledge building in discourse analysis studies of language and literacy events in classrooms has primarily occurred through dialectical processes. As such, discourse analysis studies have often been oriented to constructing, deconstructing, and reconstructing basic theoretical constructs held by a field about language and literacy events in classrooms including what counts as knowledge, reading, literacy, text, and learning; what counts as an argument, a warrant, and evidence; and what counts as a narrative and what narratives count. Third, a discourse analysis may focus on just a few minutes within a classroom event, but it does so with recognition that the classroom event is related to other events, including previous and future events, and that it is also related to social, cultural, political, and economic dynamics at broader levels. The relationships among events and levels of social context are constructed by what people do in interaction with each other over time. Fourth, the particularity of an event matters. Who is in an event and what they are doing, where, when, and how, cannot be reduced to an abstraction and still maintain the critical aspects of how the people in the event discourse the event, themselves, and the meanings and significances of the event into being. This fourth theme warrants what we earlier referred to as a "problem-based" orientation to discourse analysis studies (see introduction). We argued that the entry point to a discourse analysis study of language and literacy events in classrooms is a "problem" located in the everyday life experiences of the people in the setting itself.

These four themes can be viewed as creating a set of productive tensions among three sets of theories: the extant set of theories in the field about literacy events in classrooms, the set of theories that guide the specific approach to discourse analysis being used (what might be called the methodological warrants or logics-of-inquiry), and the implicit theories embedded in the literacy event itself and jointly held by the people involved in the classroom literacy event (see Figure 4.1).

Figure 4.1. Productive tensions among three sets of theories.

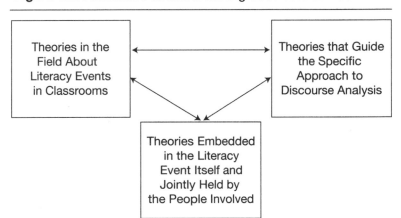

The extant set of theories in the field includes all of the established theories about the nature of reading, writing, classroom instruction, and classroom life. One of the purposes of a discourse analysis is to provide nuanced understandings that challenge extant theories, not at the level of confirming or disconfirming them, but rather in redefining terms, shifting the "footing" (cf. Goffman, 1981), and providing critical reassessments of basic concepts (cf. Potter et al., 1990). For example, discourse analysis of classroom literacy events is unlikely to confirm or disconfirm whether phonemic awareness is or is not a prerequisite to fluency in reading. Rather, discourse analysis might provide a nuanced understanding of what the lived experience of instruction in phonemic awareness is for children and teachers in actual classroom events and how they interactionally and linguistically construct what phonemic awareness and fluency are. In addition, a discourse analysis study might challenge the assumption that reading is a monolithic practice, or it might challenge definitions of phonemic awareness and fluency. Similarly, a discourse analysis study of classroom literacy events is unlikely to confirm or disconfirm whether time on task is a factor in academic achievement, but it might challenge or offer new definitions of time and what a task is and thus provoke a reconceptualization of the construct of time on task (e.g., see Bloome, Puro, & Theodorou, 1989).

A discourse analysis may also create dialectical tensions with regard to the set of theories that guide the specific approach to discourse analysis being used (the methodological warrants). That is, any research begins with a set of theories that define what knowledge is and how knowledge might be known. Researchers begin with such methodological warrants as they plan their studies. But in the course of the research, as researchers reflect on what they are finding and on how they are finding new insights and knowledge, they are liable to find that the very methodological warrants they have used are challenged. For example, consider a discourse analysis study of instructional conversations in classroom reading groups. Part of the theoretical framing guiding the study might hold that successful communication occurs when interlocutors clearly signal their intentions and when there is acknowledgement of communicative intent. The methodological warrant that follows might be to capture and transcribe how the teacher and students communicate their intentions, acknowledge each other's communicative intents, and repair communicative messages that are unclear. But if the study revealed that the teacher or students communicated ambiguous messages (or that messages were reconstructed as ambiguous) and that such ambiguity played an important role in facilitating the interactional accomplishment of the reading lesson, such a finding would require rethinking the original theoretical framing and call for methodological procedures that would foreground the analysis of ambiguity and what constituted a conversational repair (e.g., Bloome, 1993). In our experience, such reframings often occur because of a dialectical relationship between theoretical framing and the close analysis of what occurs (the material evidence) in an event.

A third set of dialectical tensions involves the implicit theories embedded in the classroom literacy event and jointly held as a working consensus by the people involved in the event. Some researchers might call the implicit theories held by the people in the event their cultural knowledge or shared cultural models. It is their implicitly held shared sense of how people should act, think, feel, believe, and use language, in various types of events, along with the broader cultural ideology, that supports such a sense (what some scholars would call their "folk theories"). For example, teachers and students have a shared sense of how their particular reading group should be conducted, how they should react to each other, what is happening, and what it means; a shared belief that it contributes to learning to read; and a shared sense that students should feel happy and proud when they are praised for their reading performances in the reading group. This shared sense of how a reading group should be conducted might be labeled their local cultural model for doing reading group. The teacher and students might justify their shared sense of reading groups by referencing theories of learning that they believe in (e.g., practice leads to learning), theories of morality (e.g., each person should have an equal number of turns), theories of human nature (e.g., motivation is the result of accountability), theories about knowledge (e.g., knowledge is given by the teacher to students who stockpile it), and so on. The theories that the people in the event hold may be in dialectical tension with the theories held by the field (e.g., scientific theories of learning, scholarly discussions of morality and human nature) and with the epistemological theories that originally framed the discourse analysis study (e.g., knowledge is socially constructed). The "folk" theories that people hold should not be assumed to be less valid than the "scientific" theories held by researchers, and thus the tension between these set of theories is not necessarily between ill-informed and informed theories. Researchers can use these dialectical tensions to reflect on the theories in the field and consider revising those theories including the social, political, and epistemological work that the theories do.

LAMINATING DISCOURSE ANALYSIS STUDIES

In the previous chapter, we provided illustrations of four different approaches to discourse analysis of language and literacy events in classrooms. Earlier in this chapter we described the relationships among these studies as parallel; they involve some similar dimensions but lack complementarity of underlying theoretical assumptions. The Smith and Goldman analyses were both concerned with how language creates opportunities for learning, but their definitions of opportunities for learning, were fundamentally different. Smith defined opportunities for learning as social

spaces for adopting and acquiring particular language practices;
Goldman defined opportunities for learning as cognitive scaffolds
for learning how to construct a textbase from a written text and a
set of textual interpretations. Macbeth and Carter were both concerned about the ethics of the event. Macbeth defined the ethics as
social relationships among the participants as they built on each
other's turns at talk and constructed the lesson. Carter defined
ethics as a historical positioning of people by gender and race and
the omission of challenges to such positioning. These analyses
are not antagonistic to each other, but whatever connections there
may be across these analyses will need to be socially constructed;
that is, the relationships will need to be interactionally proposed,
acknowledged, recognized, and have social consequence. More
simply stated, an argument for a relationship needs to be war-
ranted and accepted by others.

What can be made of these different analyses? Can they be
brought together? And, if so, how? Can they be integrated with
other forms of analyses? Do they have something to say collectively? Focusing on the same event does not necessarily provide
a rationale for laminating the four discourse analyses. Having
the four discourse analyses focus on one event was a trope we
used to highlight different approaches to discourse analyses, not
a way to address a "problem" derived from the setting or to create productive tensions with extant theories or previous studies.
The teacher and students in the ninth-grade classroom did not
experience the event as four different events, but rather simultaneously they were collectively constructing the event while also
being individuals experiencing the event—and this was accom-
plished as an indivisible whole. No matter how large the set of
studies, there is no way to capture the whole as a whole. Thinking metaphorically, consider the difference between a board that
has been made by laminating together a series of thin layers of
composite materials with a board made from a single piece of
wood: They may be of the same size and strength and they may
be put to some similar uses, but they are not the same. Similarly,
not only is a set of research studies not the same as the event itself, but also the purpose of research is not to re-create the event
but to provide knowledge and understandings that can be used
in future events.

There are several key questions to ask about any lamination
of research studies:

- What kind of a relationship is being built among research perspectives?
- By whom?
- With whom?
- For what purposes?
- When?
- Where?
- With what consequences for whom?

Such questions make clear that laminating research studies, including discourse analysis studies, is not a neutral, technical matter but a social and ideological process involving all of the complexities of human relationships (for detailed discussion, see Bloome et al., 2005).

We offer here two ways of laminating discourse analysis studies, with recognition that there are other ways of laminating discourse analysis studies and that these may also be of use in laminating other types of studies.

Laminating Based on the Contexts of Production and Consumption

In his approach to critical discourse analysis, Fairclough (1995) emphasizes the importance of examining texts within their contexts of production as well as their contexts of consumption. He suggests that texts be analyzed in terms of each of these contexts at three levels: description, interpretation, and explanation. For Fairclough, description refers to a linguistic analysis of a text, interpretation is an analysis of the relationship between the text and the contexts of production and consumption, and explanation is an analysis of social processes and power relations informed by the other two levels and by social theories.

With regard to any laminating of discourse analysis studies, one set of questions to ask would be:

- What is the context of the production of laminating the studies?
- What is the anticipated context of the consumption of the laminated studies?
- What are the relationships—social, cultural, economic, political—of the context of production and the context

of consumption and how does the laminated text reflect
and refract that relationship?

- What textual/descriptive analyses, interpretive analyses,
and explanatory analyses are afforded and foregrounded
by the contexts and processes of production and
consumption?

We can ask the questions above, for example, about the lamination of the four discourse analyses presented in Chapter 3. The
context of production includes not only the offices of the individual scholars who each contributed an analysis, but also the institutional contexts in which they work (universities) and the social
and power relations there. The context of production includes the
publisher and its corporate owners, the National Conference on
Research in Language and Literacy, the series editors, as well as
the seven authors of this book and our relationships and institutional contexts. The original data collection and data analysis (e.g.,
the transcribing) was conducted as part of a Spencer Foundation
Grant, and that too is part of the context of production. Teachers participated in the original study and their interests reflected
the positions they occupied in their school districts (the goals, demands, and conditions the district placed on them) as well as the
broader set of dynamics involved in the social institution of urban
education.

All of these contexts of production are motivated. That is, they
have an agenda they are pursuing through production and distribution of the text. Part of the dynamics also includes the anticipated contexts of consumption. Questions concern how the book
was to be positioned with regard to other research books (both
those in the series and others; note the similar titles and covers of
the books in the NCRLL series and the potential meanings that
has about diverse research methodologies), how the audience/
readership of the book was conceptualized and reflected in the
text (see the introduction), and how the four discourse analyses
would be interpreted with regard to the positioning of the book
and the audience/readership. In part, anticipation of the context
of consumption involves anticipating extant definitions of what
counts as knowledge and how the four analyses might broaden or
challenge those extant definitions. In so doing, each of the analyses is making a claim about its legitimacy as a valid and valuable

orientation to knowledge and knowing; and as a set, a similar broader claim is being made. Such a claim takes place in a political context in which the state has narrowed the range of "legitimate" approaches to knowledge (see Eisenhart & Towne, 2003), and none of the four analyses falls within that range. Thus one could view each of the analyses as related because of the challenge they pose to the state's definitions of what counts as knowledge. The analyses as a collective can also be viewed as embodying a debate between heterogeneity or homogeneity in research and between what Street (1984, 1993b) has called ideological models and autonomous models.

In brief, all laminations, including the one in this book, are rhetorical, motivated, and ideological.

Laminating Narratives

Bloome and Solsken (1992) have argued that there are two ways that narratives can be related to each other:

1. The narratives can be incorporated into one of the narratives.
2. The narratives can be brought together to create a new narrative distinct from the previous narratives.

The first of these might be called *assimilating narratives*, the second *adapting narratives*.

With regard to assimilating narratives, the lead narrative defines the purpose and theme of the narrative, the dominant framing constructs (e.g., how language is defined), its structure (both as a narrative and as an argument), what counts as pertinent knowledge, and what counts as intercontextuality (i.e., its relationship to other events and to history). If the lead narrative focuses on sociocognitive processes, then the insights located in the other narratives are reshaped (assimilated) to the goal of understanding how students acquire a set of cognitive practices. If the lead narrative focuses on the representation and experiences of black women, then insights about opportunities for learning-language practices, turn-taking practices, cognitive practices, and so forth, are reshaped (assimilated) by that frame and are incorporated into elucidating the representation and experiences of black women. Certainly, the assimilation of narratives can be abusive as occurs when the insights and findings from an analysis are distorted to mean something never intended or something inconsistent with its original theoretical framing. But it can also be the case that the assimilation of narratives can provide richer insight and depth and raise new research questions. For example, consider the assimilation of the discourse analysis on sociocognitive processes within the discourse analysis conducted from a Black Feminist perspective. New research questions might be raised about how textbases are constructed across texts and how an ethics of personhood and history might be incorporated into the cognitive practices scaffolded through instructional conversations in ways that promote ideologically reflective practices.

With regard to adapting narratives to the creation of a new narrative beyond any of the extant narratives of discourse analysis, it is impossible to give a formula for such new narratives. Bakhtin (1935/1981) suggests that new narratives are not constituted by surface-level variations, but rather by changes in how people move through time and space (which he calls "chronotopes"). Bakhtin argues that chronotopes define the nature of the protagonist. Some chronotopes frame the protagonist as moving through time and space as if the sequence of events and adventures does not matter and as if there is no change in the protagonist. Other chronotopes highlight particular aspects of change in the protagonist (e.g., maturity, the development of courage, self-insight) or in the world (e.g., the creation of more equitable social relationships). In brief, a *chronotope* is always a definition of people and the worlds in which they live. In Alice Walker's "Everyday Use," Dee (Wangero), Maggie, and their mother, all move through time and space and how they do so—how Alice Walker fashions their movement through time and space—defines who they are individually and collectively. The worlds they live in have changed and continue to change, and they are all acting on those worlds but in different ways. So, too, are the teacher and students in the ninth-grade language arts classroom. Each of the four discourse analyses have an underlying chronotope, and each defines who they are individually and collectively through how the discourse analysis constitutes their movement through time and space. A new narrative, one that brings the four analyses together will need to construct a new chronotope and incorporate the four discourse analyses into that new narrative.

FINAL COMMENTS

We began this book by locating discourse analysis of language and literacy events in classrooms in four broad frames (see Chapter 1):

1. The linguistic turn in the social sciences,
2. The foregrounding of local events and their relationships to broader cultural and social processes (i.e., micro and macro level approaches)
3. Recognition of the importance of social and historical contexts
4. Recognition that discourse processes always involve power relations.

One reason for framing discourse analysis in this way is to make clear that discourse analysis studies of language and literacy events in classrooms are part of broader intellectual agendas and that these agendas have and can have real, material consequences for people's lives. We want to make clear that what is at issue in discourse analysis studies of language and literacy events in classrooms is not fidelity to a set of methodological procedures or even to a set of theoretical constructs that might constitute a logic-of-inquiry for discourse analysis. Rather, it is these broader intellectual agendas and their potentials that is of significance for making a difference in the lives of teachers and students and other "ordinary" people in their everyday lives.

Raymond Williams (1977) wrote, "A definition of language [and we would add literacy] is always, implicitly or explicitly, a definition of human beings in the world" (p. 21). One way to view discourse analysis is as definitions of language in search of definitions of "human beings in the world."

References

Adam, B. (1990). *Time and social theory.* Philadelphia: Temple University Press.

Agar, M. (1994). *Language shock: Understanding the culture of conversation.* New York: Quill.

Atkinson, P. (1990). *The ethnographic imagination: Textual constructions of reality.* New York: Routledge.

Austin, J. (1962). *How to do things with words.* Oxford: Clarendon Press.

Bakhtin, M. (1981). Discourse in the novel. In M. Holquist (Ed. & Trans.), *The dialogic imagination* (pp. 259–422). Austin: University of Texas Press. (Original work published 1935)

Bakhtin, M. M. (1986). The problem of speech genres (V. McGee, Trans.). In C. Emerson & M. Holquist (Eds.), *Speech genres and other late essays.* Austin: University of Texas Press. (Original work published 1953)

Bakhtin, M.M., & Medvedev, P. N. (1978). *Formal method in literary scholarship: A critical introduction to sociological poetics* (A. J. Wehrle, Trans.). Baltimore: Johns Hopkins University Press. (Original work published 1928)

Banquedano-Lopez, P., Solis, J., & Kattan, S. (2005). Adaptation: The language of classroom learning. *Linguistics and Education, 16,* 1–26.

Bauman, R. (1986). *Story, performance, and event: Contextual studies of oral narrative.* New York: Cambridge University Press.

Bechely, L. (1999). *A study of the social organization of parents' work for public school choice.* Unpublished doctoral dissertation, University of California, Los Angeles.

Becker, A. (1988). Language in particular: A lecture. In D. Tannen (Ed.), *Linguistics in context* (pp. 17–35). Norwood, NJ: Ablex.

Birdwhistell, R. (1977). Some discussion of ethnography, theory, and method. In John Brockman (Ed.), *About Bateson: Essays on Gregory Bateson* (pp. 103–144). New York: Dutton.

Blackburn, M. (2005). Agency in borderland discourses: Examining language use in a community center with Black queer youth. *Teachers College Record, 107,* 89–113.

Blommaert, J., & Bulcaen, C. (2000). Critical discourse analysis. *Annual Review of Anthropology, 29,* 447–466.

Bloome, D. (1993). Necessary indeterminacy: Issues in the microethnographic study of reading as a social process. *Journal of Reading Research, 16,* 98–111.

Bloome, D., & Bailey, F. (1992). From linguistics and education, a direction for the study of language and literacy. In R. Beach, J. Green, M. Kamil, & T. Shanahan (Eds.), *Multiple disciplinary perspectives on language and literacy research* (pp. 18–210). Urbana, IL: National Conference on Research in English and National Council of Teachers of English.

Bloome, D., Carter, S. P., Christian, B. M., Otto, S., Shuart-Farris, N. (2005). *Discourse analysis and the study of classroom language and literacy events: A microethnographic perspective.* Mahwah: Erlbaum.

Bloome, D., & Clark, C. (2006). Discourse-in-use. In J. Green, G. Camilli, & P. Elmore (Eds.), *Complementary methods for research in education* (pp. 227–242). Washington, DC: American Educational Research Association.

Bloome, D., & Egan-Robertson, A. (1993). The social construction of intertextuality and classroom reading and writing. *Reading Research Quarterly, 28,* 303–333.

Bloome, D., & Goldman, S. (1999*). Reconceptualizing reading as intertextual practice*. Paper presented at the annual meeting of the American Educational Research Association, Montreal, Quebec, Canada

Bloome, D., & Katz, L. (2003). Methodologies in research on young children and literacy. In J. Larson, N. Hall, & J. Marsh (Eds.), *Handbook of early childhood literacy.* London: Sage.

Bloome, D., Puro, P., & Theodorou, E. (1989). Procedural display and classroom lessons. *Curriculum Inquiry, 19,* 265–291.

Bloome, D., & Solsken, J. (1992, March). *Beyond poststructuralism: Story and narrative in the study of literacy in the everyday world.* Paper presented at the annual convention of the Amercian Educational Research Association, San Francisco.

Bloome, D., & Talwalkar, S. (1997). Critical discourse analysis and the study of reading and writing. *Reading Research Quarterly, 32,* 104–113.

Borko, H., & Eisenhart, M. (1987). Reading ability groups as literacy communities. In D. Bloome (Ed.), *Classrooms and literacy* (pp. 107–134). Norwood, NJ: Ablex.

Bossert, S. (1979). *Tasks and social relationships in classrooms: A study of instructional organization and its consequences.* New York: Cambridge University Press.

Bourdieu, P. (1977). *Outline of a theory of practice.* New York: Cambridge University Press.

Bourdieu, P., & Thompson, J. B. (1991). *Language and symbolic power.* Cambridge, MA: Harvard University Press.

Bransford, J., Brown, A., & Cocking, R. (Eds.). (1999). *How people learn: Brain, mind, experience and school.* Washington, DC: National Academy Press.

Bransford, J., Pellegrino, J., & Donovan, S. (Eds.). (1999). *How people learn: Bridging research and practice.* Washington, DC: National Academy Press.

Candela, A. (1999). Students' power in classroom discourse. *Linguistics and Education, 10,* 139–163.

Carter, S. P. (2001). *The possibilities of silence: African-American female cultural identity and secondary English classrooms.* Unpublished doctoral dissertation. Vanderbilt University, Nashville, TN.

Christian, B., & Bloome, D. (2004). Learning to read is who you are. *Reading Writing Quarterly, 20*(4), 365–384.

Cicourel, A. V. , Jennings, K. H., Jennings, S. H. M., Leiter, K. C. W., Mac-Kay, R., Mehan, H., & Roth, D. R. (1974). *Language use and school performance.* New York: Academic Press.

Cisneros, S. (1984). *The house on Mango Street.* New York: Knopf.

Clifford, J., & Marcus, G. (Eds.). (1986). *Writing culture: The poetics and politics of ethnography.* Berkeley: University of California Press.

Coffey, A., & Atkinson, P. (1996). *Making sense of qualitative data: Complementary research.* Thousand Oaks, CA: Sage.

Collins, P. (2000). *Black feminist thought: Knowledge, consciousness, and the politics of empowerment.* (Rev. ed.) New York: Routledge.

The compact edition of the Oxford English dictionary. (1971). Oxford: Oxford University Press.

Cooper, H. (1982). Scientific guidelines for conducting integrative research reviews. *Review of Educational Research, 52,* 291–302.

Coté, N., & Goldman, S. R. (1999). Building representations of informational text: Evidence from children's think-aloud protocols. In H. Van Oostendorp & S. R. Goldman (Eds.), *The construction of mental representations during reading* (pp. 169–193). Mahwah, NJ: Erlbaum.

Coté, N., Goldman, S. R., & Saul, E. U. (1998). Students making sense of informational text: Relations between processing and representation. *Discourse Processes, 25,* 1–53.

Crusius, T. (1994). Discourse classifications (modern). In A. Purves (Ed.), *Encyclopedia of the English Language Arts* (Vol. 1, pp. 389–393). New York: Scholastic.

Cullinan, B. (1989). *Mortimer frog.* New York: Harcourt School Publishers.

De Certeau, M. (1984). *The practice of everyday life.* Berkeley: University of California Press.

Delpit, L., & Kilgour-Dowdy, J. (Eds.). (2002). *The skin that we speak: Thoughts on language and culture in the classroom.* New York: New Press.

Dewey, J. (1904). *The relation of theory to practice in education. In third year-book of the national society for the scientific study of education* (pp. 9–30). Chicago: University of Chicago Press.

Dixson, A., & Rousseau, C. (Ed.). (2005). *Critical race theory and education: All God's children got a song.* New York: Routledge.

Duranti, A. , & Goodwin, C. (Eds.). (1992). *Rethinking context: language as an interactive phenomenon.* New York: Cambridge University Press.

Eder, D. (1981). Ability grouping as a self-fulfilling prophecy: A micro-analysis of teacher–student interaction. *Sociology of Education, 54,* 151–162.

Egan-Robertson, A. (1998). Learning about culture, language, and power: Understanding relationships among literacy, personhood, and inter-textuality. *Journal of Literacy Research, 30,* 449–487.

Eisenhart, M., & Towne, L. (2003). Contestation and change in national policy on "scientifically based" education research. *Educational Researcher, 32*(7), 31–38.

Erickson, F. (2004). *Talk and social theory.* Cambridge: Polity Press.

Erickson, F., & Shultz, J. (1977). When is a context? *Newsletter of the Laboratory for Comparative Human Cognition, 1*(2), 5–12.

Fairclough, N. (1989). *Language and power.* London: Longman.

Fairclough, N. (1992). *Discourse and social change.* Cambridge, UK: Polity Press.

Fairclough, N, (1995). *Critical Discourse Analysis.* London: Longman.

Fairclough, N. (2003). *Analyzing discourse: Textual analysis for social research.* London: Routledge.

Fillmore, C. J. (1997). *Lectures on deixis.* Stanford, CA: Center for the Study of Language and Information.

Floriani, A. (1993). Negotiating what counts: Roles and relationships, texts and contexts, content and meaning. *Linguistics and Education, 5*(3), 241–274.

Foucault, M. (1965). *Madness and civilization.* New York: Vintage Books.

Foucault, M. (1972). *The archaeology of knowledge.* London: Tavistock.

Foucault, M. (1980). *Power/knowledge: Selected interviews and other writings, 1972–1977* (C. Gordon, Ed.). New York: Pantheon Books.

Frederiksen, C. (1989). Text comprehension in functional task domains. In D. Bloome (Ed.) *Classrooms and literacy* (pp. 189–232). Norwood, NJ: Ablex.

Galasinski, D. (2000). *The language of deception: A discourse analytical study.* Thousand Oaks, CA: Sage.

Garfinkel, H., & Sacks, H. (1970). On formal structures of practical actions. In J. McKinney and E. Tiryakian (Ed.), *Theoretical sociology: Perspectives and developments* (pp. 337–366). New York: Meredith.

Gee, J. P. (1996). *Social linguistics and literacies: Ideology in discourses* (2nd ed.). London: Taylor & Francis.

Geertz, C. (1973). *The interpretation of cultures.* New York: Basic Books.

Geertz, C. (1983). *Local knowledge: Further essays in interpretive anthropology.* New York: Basic Books.

Gell, A. (1992). *The anthropology of time.* Oxford: Berg.

Gergen, K. L. (1999). *An invitation to social construction.* Thousand Oaks, CA: Sage.

Giddens, A. (1979). *Central problems in social theory: Action, structure, and contradiction in social analysis.* London: Macmillan.

Gitlin, T. (Ed.). (1994). *Power and method.* London: Routledge.

Goffman, E. (1981). *Forms of talk.* Philadelphia: University of Pennsylvania Press.

Goldberg, D. (1990). (Ed.). *Anatomy of racism.* Mineapolis: University of Minnesota Press.

Goldman, S. R. (1997). Learning from text: Reflections on the past and suggestions for the future. *Discourse Processes, 23,* 357–398.

Goldman, S. R. (2003). Learning in complex domains: When and why do multiple representations help? *Learning and Instruction, 13,* 239–244.

Goldman, S. (2004). Cognitive aspects of constructing meaning through and across multiple texts. In N. Shuart-Faris & D. Bloome (Eds.), *Uses of intertextuality in classroom and educational research* (pp. 317–352). Greenwich, CT: Information Age Press.

Goldman, S. R., & Bloome, D. M. (2005). Learning to construct and integrate. In A. F. Healy (Ed.), *Experimental cognitive psychology and its applications* (pp. 169–182). Washington, DC: American Psychological Association.

González, N., Moll, L., & Amati, C. (Eds.). (2005). *Funds of knowledge: Theorizing practice in households, communities, and classrooms.* Mahwah, NJ: Erlbaum.

Goodenough, W. (1981). *Culture, language, and society.* Menlo Park, CA: Cummings.

Goodwin, C. (1981). *Conversational organization: Interaction between speakers and hearers.* New York: Academic Press.

Graesser, A. C., Gernsbacher, M. M., & Goldman, S. R. (Eds.). (2003). *Handbook of discourse processes.* Mahwah, NJ: Erlbaum.

Gray-Rosendale, L. (2000). Rethinking basic writing: Exploring identity, politics, and community in interaction. Mahwah, NJ: Erlbaum.

Green, J., & Bloome, D. (1997). Ethnography and ethnographers of and in education: A situated perspective. In J. Flood, S. Heath, & D. Lapp (Eds.), *A handbook of research on teaching literacy through the communicative and visual arts* (pp. 181–202). New York: Macmillan.

Green, J., Dixon, C. N., & Zaharlick, A. (2003). Ethnography as a logic of inquiry. In J. Flood, D. Lapp, J. R. Squire, & J. M. Jensen (Eds.), *Handbook of research on the teaching of the English language arts* (2nd ed., pp. 201–224). Mahwah, NJ: Erlbaum.

Green, J., & Wallat, C. (Eds.). (1981). *Ethnography and language in educational settings.* Norwood, NJ: Ablex.

Gumperz, J. J. (1986). *Discourse strategies.* New York: Cambridge University Press.

Gutierrez, K., & Larson, J. (1994). Language borders: Recitation as hegemonic discourse. *International Journal of Educational Reform, 3*(1), 22–36.

Habermas, J. (1984). *The theory of communicative action: Vol. 1. Reason and the rationalization of society.* London: Heinemann.

Habermas, J. (1987). *The theory of communicative action: Lifeworld and system: A critique of functionalist reason. (Vol. 2).* London: Heinemann.

Hanks, W. F. (1996). *Language and communicative practices.* Boulder, CO: Westview Press.

Heap, J. (1985). Discourse in the production of classroom knowledge: Reading lessons. *Curriculum Inquiry, 15*(3), 245–279.

Heath, S. (1982). Protean shapes in literacy events. In D. Tannen (Ed.), *Spoken and written language* (pp. 348–370). Norwood, NJ: Ablex.

Heath, S., & Street, B. (2008). *On ethnography: Approaches to language and literacy research.* New York: Teachers College Press.

Heritage, J. (1984a). A change-of-state token and aspects of its sequential placement. In J. M. Atkinson & J. C. Heritage (Eds.), *Structures of social action.* Cambridge: Cambridge University Press.

Heritage, J. (1984b). *Garfinkel and ethnomethodology.* Cambridge: Polity.

Hiebert, E. H. (1983). An examination of ability grouping for reading instruction. *Reading Research Quarterly, 18*(2), 231–255.

Higginbotham, E. (1992). African-American women's history and metalanguage of race. *Signs: Journal of Women in Culture and Society, 17,* 251–274.

Hoel, H. (n.d.). Personal names and heritage: Alice Walker's "Everyday Use." Retrieved July 15, 2008 from http://home.online.no/~helhoel/walker.htm

Holland, D., Cain, C., & Skinner, D. (1998). *Identity and agency in cultural worlds.* Cambridge MA: Harvard University Press.

Holland, D., & Quinn, N. (Eds.). (1987). *Cultural models in language and thought.* New York: Cambridge University Press.

hooks, bell. (1993). *Sisters of the yam.* Boston, MA: South End Press.

Hymes, D. (1974). *The foundations of sociolinguistics: Sociolinguistic ethnography.* Philadelphia: University of Pennsylvania Press.

Ivanic. R. (1998). *Writing and identity: The discoursal construction of identity in academic writing.* Amsterdam: John Benjamins.

Jefferson, G. (1978). Sequential aspects of storytelling in conversation. In J. Schenkein (Ed.), *Studies in the organization of conversational interaction* (pp. 219–248). New York: Academic Press.

Kaomea, J. (2003). Reading erasures and making the familiar strange: Defamiliarizing methods for research in formerly colonized and historically oppressed communities. *Educational Researcher, 32*(2), 14–23.

Karenga, M. (2005). Revisting *Brown*, reaffirming black: Reflections on race, law, and struggle. In M. Asante & M. Karenga (Ed.), *Handbook of black studies* (pp. 165–185). Thousand Oaks,CA: Sage.

Kinneavy, J. (1971). *Theory of discourse*. New York: Norton.

Kintsch, W., Britton, B. K., Fletcher, C. R., Kintsch, E., Mannes, S. M., & Nathan, M. J. (1993). A comprehension-based approach to learning and understanding. In D. L. Medin (Ed.), *The psychology of learning and motivation* (Vol. 30, pp. 165–214). New York: Academic Press.

Kulik, D., & Stroud, C. (1993). Conceptions and uses of literacy in a Papua New Guinean village. In B. Street (Ed.), *Cross-cultural approaches to literacy*. Cambridge: Cambridge University Press.

Kumashiro, K. (2001). "Posts" perspectives on anti-oppressive education in social studies, English, mathematics, and science classrooms. *Educational Researcher, 30*(4), 3–12.

Ladner, J. (1972). *Tomorrow's tomorrow: The black woman*. Garden City, NY: Doubleday.

Lakoff, G., & Johnson, M. (1980). *Metaphors we live by*. Chicago: University of Chicago Press.

Lasn, K. (2000). *Culture jam: The uncooling of America*. New York: Harper-Collins.

Lave, J. (1996). Teaching, as learning, in practice. *Mind, Culture, and Activity, 3*, 149–164.

Lave, J., & Wenger, E. (1991). *Situated learning. Legitimate peripheral participation*. Cambridge: Cambridge University Press.

Leander, K. (2004). "They took out the wrong context": Uses of time-space in the practice of positioning. *Ethnos, 32*, 188–213.

Leander, K., & Sheehy, M. (Eds.). (2004). *Spatializing literacy research and practice*. New York: Peter Lang.

Lee, Y. A. (2004). The work of examples in classroom instruction. *Linguistics and Education, 15*, 99–120.

Lemke, J. (1995). *Textual politics: Discourse and social dynamics*. London: Taylor & Francis.

Letts, B. (2004). *Where the heart is*. New York: Grand Central.

Levinson, S. (1983). *Pragmatics*. London: Cambridge University Press.

Lewis, C. (2001). *Literacy practices as social acts: Power, status, and cultural norms in the classroom*. Mahwah, NJ: Erlbaum.

Lorde, A. (1984). *Sister outsider: Essays and speeches*. Ithaca, NY: Crossing Press.

Luke, A. (1996). Genres of power? Literacy education and the production of capital. In R. Hasan & G. Williams (Eds.), *Literacy in society*. London: Longman.

Macbeth, D. (1991). Teacher authority as practical action. *Linguistics and Education, 3*, 281–314.

Macbeth, D. (2000). Classrooms as installations. In S. Hester & J. Hughes (Eds.), *The local education order* (pp. 21–72). Amsterdam: John Benjamins.

Macbeth, D. (2003). Hugh Mehan's "Learning Lessons" reconsidered: On the difference between the naturalistic and critical analysis of classroom discourse. *American Educational Research Journal, 40*, 239–280.

Mahiri, J. (2004). New teachers for new times: The dialogic principle in teaching and learning electronically. In A. Ball & S. Freedman (Eds.), *Bakhtinian perspectives on language, literacy, and learning* (pp. 213–231). New York: Cambridge University Press.

Mayer, M. (1987). *There's an alligator under my bed*. New York: Penguin Puffin

McDermott, R. (1977). Social relations as contexts for learning in school. *Harvard Educational Review, 47*(2), 198–213.

McHoul, A. (1978). The organization of turns at formal talk in the classroom. *Language and Society, 7*, 183–213.

McHoul, A. (2001). Discourse. In R. Mesthrie (Ed.), *Concise encyclopedia of sociolinguistics* (pp. 133–144). Amsterdam: Pergamon.

Mehan, H. (1974). Accomplishing classroom lessons. In A. Cicourel et al. (Eds.), *Language use and school performance* (pp. 76–142). New York: Academic Press.

Mehan, H. (1978). Structuring school structure. *Harvard Educational Review, 48*, 32–64.

Mehan, H. (1979). *Learning lessons*. Cambridge, MA: Harvard University Press.

Mishler, E. G. (1986). *Research interviewing: Context and narrative*. Cambridge, MA: Harvard University Press.

Mishler, E. G. (1991). Representing discourse: The rhetoric of transcription. *Journal of Narrative and Life History, 1*(4), 255–280.

Mitchell, J. C. (1984). Typicality and the case study. In R. Ellen (Ed.), *Ethnographic research: A guide to general conduct* (pp. 238–241). New York: Academic Press.

Moerman, M., & Sacks, H. (1988). On "Understanding" in the analysis of natural conversation. In M. Moerman, *Talking culture* (pp. 180–186). Philadelphia: University of Pennsylvania Press. (Original paper presented 1971)

Morrison, T. (1992). *Playing in the dark: Whiteness and the literary imagination*. Cambridge, MA: Harvard University Press.

Noblit, G., & Hare, D. W. (1988). *Meta-ethnography: Synthesizing qualitative studies*. Thousand Oaks, CA: Sage.

Norris, S., & Jones, R. (2005). *Discourse in action: Introducing mediated discourse analysis*. New York: Routledge.

Nystrand, M., Gamoran, A., Kachur, R., & Prendergast, C. (1997). *Opening dialogue: Understanding the dynamics of language and learning in the English classroom*. New York: Teachers College Press.

Ochs, E. (1979). Transcription as theory. In E. Ochs & B. B. Schieffelin (Eds.), *Developmental pragmatics* (pp. 43–72). New York: Academic Press.

Payne, G., & Hustler, D. (1980). Teaching the class: The practical management of a cohort. *British Journal of Sociology of Education, 1*(1), 49–66.

Potter, J., Wetherell, M., Gill, R., & Edwards, D. (1990). Discourse: noun, verb, or social practice? *Philosophical Psychology, 3*(2), 205–217.

Punday, D. (2000). The narrative construction of cyberspace: Reading *Neuromancer*, reading cyberspace debates. *College English, 63*(2), 194–213.

Reisigl, M., & Wodak, R. (2001). *Discourse and discrimination: Rhetorics of racism and anti-Semitism*. London: Routledge.

Rex, L. A., & Green, J. L. (2008). Classroom discourse and interaction, reading across the traditions. In B. Spolsky & F. Hult (Eds.), *International handbook of educational linguistics* (pp. 571–584). London: Blackwell.

Rorty, R. (Ed.). (1967). *The linguistic turn: Essays in philosophical method*. Chicago: University of Chicago Press.

Rogers, R. (Ed.). (2004). *An introduction to critical discourse analysis in education*. Mahwah, NJ: Erlbaum.

Rogoff, B. (2003). *The cultural nature of human development*. Oxford: Oxford University Press.

Sacks, H. (1992). *Lectures on conversation*. (G. Jefferson, Ed., Volumes 1–2). Oxford: Blackwell.

Sacks, H., Schegloff, E., & Jefferson, G. (1974). A simplist systematics for the organization of turn-taking in conversation. *Language, 50*, 696–735.

Said, E. (1979). *Orientalism*. New York: Vintage Books.

Said, E. (1985). *Orientalism* reconsidered. In F. Barker, P. Hulme, M. Iversen, & D. Loxley (Eds.), *Europe and its others: Proceedings of the Essex conference on the sociology of literature* (Vol. 1, pp. 14–27). Colchester, UK: University of Essex.

Schiffrin, D. (1987). *Discourse markers*. New York: Cambridge University Press.

Schiffrin, D. (2006). *In other words: Variation in reference and narrative*. New York: Cambridge University Press.

Sfard, A., & Prusak, A. (2005). Telling identities: In search of an analytic tool for investigating learning as a culturally shaped activity. *Educational Researcher, 34*(4), 14–22.

Shuman, A. (1997). *Storytelling Rights*. New York: Cambridge University Press.

Silverstein, M., & Urban, G. (1996). The natural history of discourse. In M. Silverstein & G. Urban (Eds.), *Natural histories of discourse*. Chicago: University of Chicago Press.

Slavin, R. E. (1993). Ability grouping in the middle grades: Achievement effects and alternatives. The Elementary School Journal, 93(5), Special issue: *Middle Grades Research and Reform*, 535–552.

Smith, D. (1987). *The everyday world as problematic: A feminist sociology*. Boston: Northeastern University Press.

Soja, E. W. (1996). *Thirdspace: Journeys to Los Angeles and other real-and-imagined places*. Cambridge, MA: Blackwell.

Street, B. (1984). *Literacy in theory and practice*. New York: Cambridge University Press.

Street, B. (1993a). Culture is a verb. In D. Graddol, L. Thompson, & M. Byram (Eds.), *Language and culture* (pp. 23–42). Clevedon: Multilingual Matters/British Association of Applied Linguists.

Street, B. (1993b). Introduction. In B. Street (Ed.), *Cross-cultural approaches to literacy*. Cambridge: Cambridge University Press.

Street, B. (1995). *Social literacies: Critical approaches to literacy in development, ethnography and education*. London: Longman.

Street, B. (1996). Academic literacies. In D. Baker, C. Fox, & J. Clay (Eds.), *Challenging ways of knowing: In English, mathematics, and science* (pp. 101–106). Brighton, UK: Falmer Press.

Street, B. (2003). What's "new" in new literacy studies? Critical approaches to literacy in theory and practice. *Current Issues in Comparative Education, 5*(2), 77–91. Retrieved December 29, 2007 from http://www.tc.columbia.edu/cice/Archives/5.2/52street.pdf.

Street, B., & Street, J. (1991). The schooling of literacy. In D. Barton & R. Ivanic (Eds.), *Writing in the community* (pp. 143–166). London: Sage.

Tannen, D. (2007). *Talking voices: Repetition, dialogue, and imagery in conversational discourse*. Cambridge: Cambridge University Press.

Titscher, S., Meyer, M., Wodak, R., & Vetter, E. (2000). *Methods of text and discourse analysis*. Thousand Oaks, CA: Sage.

Torfing, J. (1999). *New theories of discourse: Laclau, Mouffe and Žižek*. Oxford: Blackwell.

Tracy, K. (1995). Action-implicative discourse analysis. *Journal of Language and Social Psychology, 14*(1–2), 195–215.

Tylor, E. B. (1958). *Primitive culture*. New York: Harper. (Original work published 1871)

Van Dijk, T. A. (Ed.). (1997). *Discourse as structure and process*. London: Sage.

Van Dijk, T.A., & Kintsch, W. (1983). *Strategies of discourse comprehension*. San Diego, CA: Academic Press.

Volosinov, V. (1973). *Marxism and the philosophy of language* (L. Matejka & I. Titunik, Trans.). Cambridge, MA: Harvard University Press. (Original work published 1929)

Vygotsky, L. (1987). Thinking and speech. In R. Rieber & A. Carton (Eds.), *The collected works of L. S. Vygotsky: Vol 1. The problems of general psychology* (N. Minick, Trans.; pp. 39–288). New York: Plenum Press.

Wade-Gayles, G. (1997). *No crystal stair.* Cleveland, OH: Pilgrim Press.

Walker, A. (1973). Everyday use. In In love and trouble. New York: Harcourt Brace Jovanovich. Retrieved December 29, 2007, from http://xroads.virginia.edu/~ug97/quilt/walker.html.

Walkerdine, V. (1990). *Schoolgirl fictions.* London: Verso.

Washington, M. (1994). An essay on Alice Walker. In A. Walker, *Everyday use* (B. Christian, Ed., pp. 85–104). New Brunswick, NJ: Rutgers University Press.

Wertsch, J. (1993). *Voices of the mind.* Cambridge, MA: Harvard University Press.

Widdowson, H. G. (2004). *Text, context, pretext: Critical issues in discourse analysis.* Madden, MA: Blackwell.

Williams, R. (1977). *Marxism and literature.* Oxford: Oxford University Press.

Wittgenstein, L. (1958). *Philosophical investigations.* (G. E. M. Anscombe, Trans.; 3rd ed.). New York: Macmillan.

Wodak, R. (1996). *Disorders of discourse.* London: Longman.

Wolf, F. (1986). *Meta-analysis: Quantitative methods for research synthesis.* Thousand Oaks, CA: Sage.

Wortham, S. (2006). *Learning identity: The joint emergence of social identification and academic learning.* New York: Cambridge University Press.

Young, R. (1992). *Critical theory and classroom talk.* Clevedon, UK: Multilingual Matters.

Supplemental Bibliographies

Select List of Introductory Books and Handbooks on Discourse Analysis

Blommaert, J. (2005). *Discourse: A critical introduction*. Cambridge: Cambridge University Press.

Bloome, D., Carter, S. P., Christian, B. M., Otto, S., & Shuart-Faris, N. (2005). *Discourse analysis and the study of classroom language and literacy events: A microethnographic perspective*. Mahwah, NJ: Erlbaum

Cameron, D. (2001). *Working with spoken discourse*. Thousand Oaks, CA: Sage.

Christie, F. (2002). *Classroom discourse analysis: A functional perspective*. New York: Continuum.

Cole, K., & Zuengler, J. (Eds.). (2008). *The research process in classroom discourse analysis: Current perspectives*. New York: Erlbaum.

Coulthard, M. (1977). *An introduction to discourse analysis*. London: Longman.

Erickson, F. (2004). *Talk and social theory*. Cambridge: Polity Press.

Fairclough, N. (2003). *Analysing discourse: Textual analysis for social research*. London: Routledge.

Gee, J. P. (2005). *An introduction to discourse analysis: Theory and method* (2nd ed.). New York: Routledge.

Graesser, A. C., Gernsbacher, M. A., & Goldman, S. R. (Eds.). (2003). *Handbook of discourse processes*. Mahwah, NJ: Erlbaum.

Green, J., & Wallat, C. (Eds). (1981). *Ethnography and language in educational settings*. Norwood, NJ: Ablex.

Howarth, D. (2000). *Discourse*. Philadelphia: Open University Press.

Jaworski, A., & Coupland, N. (1999). *The discourse reader*. London: Routledge.

Johnstone, B. (2008). *Discourse analysis* (2nd ed.). Malden, MA: Blackwell.

McDonell, D. (1986). *Theories of discourse: An introduction*. Oxford: Blackwell.

McHoul, A. W., & Rapley, M. (2001). *How to analyse talk in institutional settings : a casebook of methods*. London: Continuum.

Mills, S. (2004). *Discourse.* London: Routledge.

Norris, S., & Jones, R. (2005). *Discourse in action: Introducing mediated discourse analysis.* New York: Routledge.

Paltridge, B. (2006). *Discourse analysis.* New York: Continuum.

Phillips, N., & Hardy, C. (2002). *Discourse analysis: Investigating processes of social construction.* Thousand Oaks, CA: Sage.

Rogers, R. (Ed.). (2004). *An introduction to critical discourse analysis in education.* Mahwah, NJ: Erlbaum.

Schiffrin, D. (1994). *Approaches to discourse.* Cambridge, MA: Blackwell.

Schiffrin, D., Tannen, D., & Hamilton, H. E. (2001). *The handbook of discourse analysis.* Malden, MA: Blackwell.

Titscher, S. (2000). *Methods of text and discourse analysis.* Thousand Oaks, CA: Sage.

Toolan, M. J. (2002). *Critical discourse analysis: Critical concepts in linguistics.* London ; New York: Routledge.

Van Dijk, T. A. (Ed.) (2001). *Discourse as social interaction.* Thousand Oaks, CA: Sage.

Van Dijk, T. A. (Ed.) (1997). *Discourse as structure and process.* London: Sage.

Van Dijk, T. A. (Ed.) (1985) *Handbook of discourse analysis* (Vols. 1–4). London: Academic Press.

Walsh, S. (2006). *Investigating classroom discourse.* New York: Routledge.

Weiss, G., & Wodak, R. (2003). *Critical discourse analysis: Theory and interdisciplinarity.* New York: Palgrave Macmillan.

Widdowson, H. G. (2004). *Text, context, pretext: Critical issues in discourse analysis.* Malden, MA: Blackwell.

Wood, L., & Kroger, R. O. (2000). *Doing discourse analysis: Methods for studying action in talk and text.* Thousand Oaks, CA: Sage.

Woods, N. (2006). *Describing discourse: A practical guide to discourse analysis.* New York: Hodder Arnold.

Select List of Discourse Analysis Studies of Language and Literacy in Classrooms

Adger, C. T. (1998). Register shifting with dialect resources in instructional discourse. In S. Hoyle & C. T. Adger (Eds.), *Kids talk: Strategic language use in later childhood* (pp. 151–169). New York: Oxford University Press.

Bannink, A., & Van Dam, J. (2006). A dynamic discourse approach to classroom research. *Linguistics and Education, 17,* 283–301.

Carter, S. P. (2007). "Reading all that crazy white stuff": Black young women unpacking whiteness in a high school British literature classroom. *Journal of Classroom Interaction, 41*(2), 42–55.

Cazden, C, John, V., & Hymes, D. (Eds.). (1972). *Functions of language in the classroom.* New York: Teachers College Press.

Christie, F. (1995). Pedagogic discourse in the primary school. *Linguistics and Education, 7,* 221–242.

Cochran-Smith, M. (1984). *The making of a reader.* Norwood, NJ: Ablex.

Cole, K., & Zuengler, J. (Eds.) (2008). *The research process in classroom discourse analysis: Current perspectives.* New York: Erlbaum.

Collins, J. (1996). Socialization to text: Structure and contradiction in schooled literacy. In M. Silverstein & G. Urban (Eds.), *Natural histories of discourse* (pp. 203–228). Chicago: University of Chicago Press.

DaSilva Iddings, A. C. (2007). Integrating home and school identities of recent-immigrant Hispanic English language learners through classroom practice. *Journal of Language, Identity and Education, 6*(4), 299–314.

Davies, B. (1983). The role pupils play in the social construction of classroom order. *British Journal of Sociology of Education, 4*(1), 55–69.

Dorr-Bremme, D. W. (1990). Contextualization cures in the classroom: Discourse regulation and social control functions. *Language in Society, 19*(3), 379–402.

Duff, P. (2004). Intertextuality and hybrid discourses: The infusion of pop culture in educational discourse. *Linguistics and Education, 14,* 231–276.

Floriani, A. (1993). Negotiating what counts: Roles and relationships, texts and contexts, content and meaning. *Linguistics and Education, 5,* 241–274.

Foster, M. (1995). Talking that talk: The language of control, curriculum, and critique. *Linguistics and Education, 7,* 129–150.

Freitas, C. A., & Castanheira, M. L. (2007). Talked images: Examining the contextualised nature of image use. *Pedagogies, 2*(3) 151–164.

Godley, A., Carpenter, B., & Werner, C. (2007). "I'll speak in proper slang": Language ideologies in a daily editing activity. *Reading Research Quarterly, 42,* 100–131.

Goldenberg, C., & Pathey-Chavez, G. (1995). Discourse processes in instructional conversations: Interactions between teacher and transition readers. *Discourse Processes, 19,* 57–73.

Goldman, S. R., & Bloome, D. M. (2005). Learning to construct and integrate. In A. F. Healy (Ed.), *Experimental cognitive psychology and its applications* (pp. 169–182). Washington, DC: American Psychological Association.

Green, J., & Dixon, C. (1993). Talking knowledge into being: Discursive and social practices in classrooms. *Linguistics and Education, 5,* 231–239.

He, A. W. (2001). The language of ambiguity: Practices in Chinese language classes. *Discourse Studies, 3,* 75–96.

Heap, J. L. (1985). Discourse in the production of classroom knowledge: Reading lessons. *Curriculum Inquiry, 15*(3), 245–279.

Heras, A. (1993). The construction of understanding in a sixth-grade bilingual classroom. *Linguistics and Education, 5,* 275–300.

Hicks, D. (Ed.). (1996). *Discourse, learning, and schooling.* Cambridge: Cambridge University Press.

Higgins, C. M., Thompson, M. M., & Roeder, R. V. (2003). In search of a profound answer: Mainstream scripts and the marginalization of advanced-track urban students. *Linguistics and Education, 14,* 195–220.

Ivanic, R. (1994). I is for interpersonal: Discoursal construction of writer identities and the teaching of writing. *Linguistics and Education, 6,* 3-15.

Kamberelis, G. (2001). Producing of heteroglossic classroom (micro)cultures through hybrid discourse practice. *Linguistics and Education, 12,* 85–125.

Kantor, R., Green, J. L., Bradley, M., & Lin, L. (1992). The construction of schooled discourse repertoires: An interactional sociolinguistic perspective on learning to talk in preschool. *Linguistics and Education, 4,* 131–172.

Larson, J. (1995). Talk matters: The role of pivot in the distribution of literacy knowledge among novice writers. *Linguistics and Education, 7,* 277–302.

Leander, K. (2002). Silencing in classroom interaction: Producing and relating social spaces. *Discourse Process, 34,* 193–235.

Lee, Y. (2007). Third turn position in teacher talk: Contingency and the work of teaching. *Journal of Pragmatics, 39,* 1204–1230.

Lewis, C. (2001). *Literacy practices as social acts: Power, status, and cultural norms in the classroom.* Mahwah, NJ: Erlbaum.

Love, K. (2000). The regulation of argumentative reasoning in pedagogic discourse. *Discourse Studies, 2,* 420–451.

Mariage, T. V. (2000). Constructing educational possibilities: A sociolinguistic examination of meaning-making in "sharing chair." *Learning Disability Quarterly, 23*(2) 79–103.

Marton, F., & Tsui, A. B. M. (Eds.). (2004). *Classroom discourse and the space of learning.* Mahwah, NJ: Erlbaum.

Maybin, J. (2006). *Children's voices: Talk, knowledge, and identity.* Basingstoke, UK: Palgrave.

Mehan, H. (1979). *Learning lessons.* Cambridge, MA: Harvard University Press.

Mercer, N. (2000). *Words and minds.* New York: Routledge.

Mori, J. (2002). Task design, plan, and development of talk-in-interaction: An analysis of a small group activity in a Japanese language classroom. *Applied Linguistics, 23*(3), 323–347.

O'Conner, M. C., & Michaels, S. (1993). Aligning academic task and participation status through revoicing: Analysis of a classroom discourse strategy. *Anthropology and Education Quarterly, 24*(4), 318–335.

Pappas, C. C., & Varelas, M. (2004). Dialogic inquiry around information texts: The role of intertextuality in constructing scientific understandings in urban primary classrooms. In N. Shuart-Faris & D. Bloome (Eds.), Uses of intertextuality in classroom and educational research (pp. 93–145). Greenwich, CT: Information Age Press.

Poole, D. (2003). Linguistic connections between co-occurring speech and writing in a classroom literacy event. *Discourse Processes, 35,* 103–134.

Poveda, D. (2003). Paths to participation in classroom conversations. *Linguistics and Education, 14,* 69–98.

Rampton, B. (2006). *Language in late modernity: Interaction in an urban school.* Cambridge: Cambridge University Press.

Rex, L., & McEachen, D. (1999). "If anything is odd, inappropriate, confusing, or boring, it's probably important": The emergence of inclusive academic literacy through English classroom discussion practices. *Research in the Teaching of English, 34*(1), 65–127.

Rockwell, E. (2000). Teaching genres: A Bakhtinian approach. *Anthropology and Education Quarterly, 31*(3), 260–282.

Scollon, R., & Scollon, S. W. (2001). Intercultural communication: A discourse approach. (2nd ed.). Malden, MA: Blackwell.

Shuart-Faris, N. (2004). Problematizing and textualizing language and race in the construction of intertextuality in a seventh grade language arts classroom. In N. Shuart-Faris & D. Bloome (Eds.), *Uses of intertextuality in classroom and educational research* (pp. 65–91). Greenwich, CT: Information Age Press.

Sterponi, L. (2007). Clandestine interactional reading: Intertextuality and double-voicing under the desk. *Linguistics and Education, 18,* 1–23.

Tholander, M. (2003). Pupils' gossip as remedial action. *Discourse Studies, 5,* 101–128.

Tuyay, S., Jennings, L., & Dixon, C. (1995). Classroom discourse and opportunities to learn: Ethnographic study of knowledge construction in a bilingual third-grade classroom. *Discourse Processes, 19,* 75–110.

Vine, E. (2003). "My partner": A five-year-old Samoan boy learns how to participate in class through interactions with his English-speaking peers. *Linguistics and Education, 14,* 99–121

Wenger, K. J., & Ernst-Slavit, G. (1999). Learning to teach in a linguistic market: Consequences of preservice Spanish teachers' different "ways with words" in an elementary school practicum. *Journal of Classroom Interaction, 34*(2), 45–57.

Willett, J., Solsken, J., & Wilson-Keenan, J. (1998). The (im)possibilities of constructing multicultural language practices in research and pedagogy. *Linguistics and Education, 10,* 165–218.

Index

About the Authors
and the Contributors

David Bloome is Professor of Education in the School of Teaching and Learning of The Ohio State University's College of Education and Human Ecology. Bloome's research focuses on how people use spoken and written language for learning in classroom and nonclassroom settings and how people use language to create and maintain social relationships, construct knowledge, and create communities, social institutions, and shared histories and futures.

Stephanie Power Carter is Associate Professor at Indiana University, Bloomington, in the Language Education Department. Her research interests include a range of topics such as Black education, silence, critical literacy, sociolinguistics, critical discourse analysis, Black feminist theory, critical race theory, and Black women's literature.

Beth Morton Christian is Associate Professor of Education at Tennessee State University. Christian works closely with preservice teachers to prepare them to teach literacy and the language arts in today's diverse classrooms. Christian's research interests involve examining social, cultural, linguistic, and political factors that influence and affect the interactions that take place among teachers and students, as well as the implications such research may have for preservice teacher education and the academic success of young students.

Susan R. Goldman is Distinguished Professor of Psychology and Education at the University of Illinois at Chicago and codirects the Center for the Study of Learning, Instruction, and Teacher Development and the Learning Sciences Research Institute. Her research focuses on learning, instruction, and assessment in classroom and nonclassroom settings and ways that technology can support them. She uses discourse analysis as a technique for revealing processes of meaning construction and understanding in individuals and groups. She applies her work to professional development in subject matter areas including literacy, mathematics, and science.

Douglas Macbeth is Associate Professor at The Ohio State University, where he studies structures of classroom interaction, discourse, and instruction. Recent work has taken special interest in instruction in the early grades and the tasks of teaching those who profoundly do not know their curriculum.

Samara Madrid is Assistant Professor in the College of Education at Northern Illinois University, where she studies young children's narrative development, emotional themes, and peer culture. Her research also explores how emotion affects language use and classroom communication among teachers and children in early childhood settings.

Sheila Otto is Associate Professor and Coordinator of the Stretch English Program at Middle Tennessee State University. Her research focuses on undergraduate basic and developmental writing; she is particularly interested in the social construction of identity in composition classrooms.

Nora Shuart-Faris is an independent scholar in Chattanooga, Tennessee. She received her Ph.D. in language and literacy from Vanderbilt University. Her research interests include how teachers of English use reading and writing in their classrooms as well as their own lives, and how the notion of intertextuality is utilized in classroom and educational research.

Mandy Smith is an independent scholar in Newark, Ohio. Areas of interest include language, literacy and culture, discourse analysis, adolescent literacy, critical pedagogies, and urban education.